**PRINT CASEBOOKS 4/1980-81 EDITION**
**THE BEST IN EXHIBITION DESIGN**

# Print Casebooks 4

# 1980/81 Edition
# The Best in Exhibition Design

Conceived by
**Martin Fox**

Text and Introduction by
**Edward K. Carpenter**

Published by
**RC Publications, Inc.**
**Washington, D.C.**

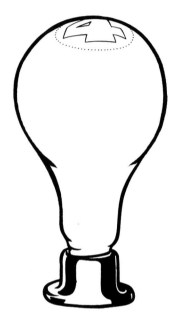

Published by RC Publications, Inc.
6400 Goldsboro Road NW
Washington, D.C. 20034

Manufactured in U.S.A
First Printing 1980

**PRINT CASEBOOKS 4/1980-81 EDITION/THE BEST IN EXHIBITION DESIGN**
Library of Congress Catalog Card Number 76-39580
ISBN 0-915734-30-3

**PRINT CASEBOOKS 4/1980-81 EDITION**
Complete 6-Volume Set
ISBN 0-915734-26-5

**RC PUBLICATIONS**
President and Publisher: Robert Cadel
Vice President and Editor: Martin Fox
Art Director/Designer: Andrew P. Kner
Associate Editor: Teresa Reese
Associate Art Director: Rose M. DeNeve
Assistant Editor: Dorian Rogers
Business Manager: Howard Cadel
Title Page Illustration: Isadore Seltzer

The 27 exhibits shown in this book appeared originally in a host of habitats. Though most of the exhibits were designed for museums, others showed up in bank lobbies, subways, trade show lofts, in a student lounge, a university art gallery, on board a train, and under a tent in a London park. None of these spots are unlikely ones; for an exhibit's logical location is anywhere people can congregate, or be made to congregate, to view it. I mention the disparity of habitats only because a quick glance at this book might lead one to think that today's exhibits appear only in museums. Indeed, 16 of the 27 seen here were sheltered by museums, and museums are, as they should be, unusually active in gathering, designing and presenting exhibits. But the point is that in the midst of the current flurry of museum exhibit activity, exhibits are flourishing elsewhere, too, perhaps bolstered by the influence museums are having on the exhibit-design profession and on the public.

The chords struck by special museum exhibits have been swelling to a crescendo since the passing of "Treasures of Tutankhamun," which toured the U.S. for two years. Even before that, museum directors were beginning to recognize that large special exhibits could bolster membership, fill museum coffers with fees paid by eager crowds, awaken public awareness in museums and, not incidentally, bring into the museum hordes of visitors who were unlikely ever to visit a museum without the publicity and excitement surrounding a major exhibit. Not too many years ago, a good deal was heard about getting exhibits out of the museum and into the surrounding community. If heard at all today, these suggestions are muted. Cities encourage these exhibits, too, for in many cases they bolster tourism. One study found that during one four-month period, the Tut exhibit alone generated $69.4 million in food, hotel, and entertainment expenditures.

According to the American Museum of Natural History, its membership doubled from 9,000 to 18,000 during the run of "Pompeii A.D. 79" (page 69). Boston's Museum of Fine Arts, where the Pompeii exhibit played with a slightly different format, attracted more visitors in four months than the museum had attracted in an entire one-year period. The "Splendors of Dresden" attracted 617,000 visitors in three months at the National Gallery of Art. And the attention heaped on museums by these exhibits makes it easier for them to solicit funds from city and state governments, from foundations, from corporations and other sources. So huge, special exhibits will no doubt be a museum fixture for a long while to come (although the new directors of the Metropolitan Museum of Art have proclaimed a policy of cutting back on blockbuster exhibits). Of these special exhibits, the large, splashy international exhibits are the most popular, and four of them appear in these pages: "Splendors of Dresden," "Golden Treasures of Peru"; "Pompeii A.D. 79"; and "Treasures from the Kremlin."

With more money for and interest in exhibitions, it is unquestionably a good time to be an exhibit designer. For one thing, the designer's importance in the success of an exhibit is becoming more widely recognized. For another, designers have a broader range of projects to work on. For some designers, especially those in major museums, the rewards of increased exhibit activity — increased budgets and responsibility, opportunities for foreign travel and friendships — have been accompanied by increasingly hectic days.

Much U.S. design today shows its debt to Charles Eames, who died during the summer of 1978 at age 72. Eames's exhibits, designed with his wife, Ray, and a number of distinguished colleagues and consultants, were cornucopias overflowing with objects, films, texts and hardware. Eames's exhibits demanded much of a viewer but left him with much if he met the demands. Somewhat in the Eames vein are the second phase of the Metropolitan's Egyptian Collection display (page 46); "Pompeii A.D. 79" (page 69); Southern Illinois University's student show (page 30); and the Smithsonian's Hall of Maritime Enterprises (page 22). Perhaps even the Metropolitan's costume shows (page 58) owe something to Eames.

But Eames's exhibits were always more than mere displays. Like the Metropolitan's Egyptian Collection and the American Museum's "Pompeii A.D. 79," his exhibits were also teaching devices. He wanted to leave visitors with a very particular insight into his exhibit's subjects. And because of this emphasis, it might well be that, of the exhibits reviewed here, Eames might have found the most pleasure in "The Money Center" (page 37), which the Burdick Group designed for the Continental Illinois National Bank. Though it lacks the crammed look of an Eames exhibit, "The Money Center" has plenty of artifacts, and most important, it teaches the visitor something about economics. It also goes beyond traditional exhibit techniques by using pinball machines and automated puppets to captivate audiences and put across its points. A computer whose terminals the Burdick Group spotted through the exhibit gives visitors a simulated bank account and helps them increase or decrease it as they move through the Center. In the use of a computer, which Eames experimented with on a smaller scale in the IBM pavilion at the 1964-65 World's Fair, "The Money Center" moves beyond most current exhibits. The computer becomes a device allowing visitors to participate in the exhibit, making their visit especially personal.

The notion of personal involvement has caused some exhibits to move away from traditional passive display. At the Brooklyn Children's Museum (page 16) a slew of ingenious devices let visitors dam streams, grind grain, run steam engines, and otherwise do things they might not do at home. And it may be that exhibits will move increasingly toward greater visitor participation.

Some experts believe that people, especially young people, learn more readily by participation than by reading or staring. If so, teaching exhibits stand to gain most from an audience's tactile involvement. Further, if an exhibit offers a visitor something to grab, play with, or manipulate, it will probably hold his attention more fully than an object or text that he can examine only visually.

Casebook Jurors

Participation will also keep him involved longer, and corporate exhibits, competing with other corporate exhibits for visitors' attention and time, can obviously profit from such physical participation.

But if exhibits are changing, they are also staying the same; the small-artifact exhibit is still very much a part of contemporary culture. But in the best of these shows the sophistication of their arrangement is becoming increasingly apparent. In at least three of these exhibits, shown here, the Casebook jurors were struck by the precision and beauty of the artifacts' arrangement, and talks with the designers of these shows revealed that while each designer relied on instinctive feelings in arranging artifacts, each, too, had definite guidelines. For example, Dextra Frankel, one of the designers of the "Overglaze Imagery" exhibit (page 94), says that she arranges small artifacts according to their chronology or geography. But within these broader frameworks, her juxtapositions are totally esthetic. "A drab object," she says, "can be made to seem more beautiful by what is next to it and by the space allowed it." Much of her emphasis contrives to make each object stand out, soliciting attention in a crowd. "Viewers," Frankel maintains, "tend to look at rows of objects from left to right. So the weight of these objects becomes important. If you have a lighter object on the right, it will fall off, seem to disappear." Similarly an object's hue determines its placement. "If a pale-colored object is to the right, it will fade out as you move your eyes to it from the left."

Frankel and her co-designer, Thomas Hartman, separated objects with different textures lest they seem to run together. And they tried to avoid grouping objects of the same color. These rules, Frankel stresses, are not irrevocable. In one show, she says, she had several vibrant green objects scattered among other pieces. Arranged this way, the green pieces seemed to jump out, to jar. Only when grouped did their intensity fade.

Both Donald Skinner, who designed the Field Museum's installation of an addition to the traveling "Golden Treasures of Peru" exhibit (page 91), and Clifford Abrams, also of the Field Museum, who designed the "Feather Arts" show (page 32), stress the importance of treating each vitrine, each showcase, as a space to be sculptured. Each of these designers brought small objects within showcases up to eye level, positioned bigger objects in back and tried to make all objects visible from all angles.

Fads in exhibit design, as elsewhere, wax and wane. Waning is the use of Helvetica typeface in texts and captions. In the exhibits seen here five (of 27) use Helvetica, down from 10 of 24 in Casebook 3. And some wonderfully appropriate type is beginning to show up in specific installations, such as the Optima that Lucian J. Leone used in the Metropolitan Museum's "Treasures from the Kremlin" and the stencil face used in the Smithsonian's Hall of American Maritime Enterprise. In general, typefaces are becoming a design element, are being given more than reflex consideration. Some designers have begun using more than one typeface per exhibit, suiting the type to the portion of the exhibit it serves,

the way gourmets select wine according to the course it accompanies.

Waxing as a potential fad is the use of plants. In an exhibit plants can create a mood, serve as dividers and screens, provide harmonious color and texture, fill blank spaces, and set scale. They were used for all these purposes in three of these exhibits: "Golden Treasures of Peru," "Pompeii A.D. 79," and "Treasures from the Kremlin." At the Field Museum, the design department has worked out an arrangement with the building maintenance department: the design department buys and uses the plants; the building staff stores and cares for them.

Judging from the exhibits seen here, it is altogether possible to design as good, if less elaborate, an exhibit on a small budget as on a large one. California's Communication Arts Society spent only $800 on their simple, nicely arranged annual show (page 88). So did the students at Southern Illinois University. On the other hand, at least half the exhibits here cost more than $100,000. And even for $2,000,000 the Metropolitan Museum of Art did a fine job with the second phase of its Egyptian Collection reinstallation.
—*Edward K. Carpenter*

The principal in Charles B Froom/Design, Brooklyn, New York, a firm which is involved primarily in fine arts installations for museums, galleries and private collections, Froom has a broad background in many phases of the museum profession, much of it received while working in graphics, design and installation — both on staff and freelance — at the Brooklyn Museum and the Museum of Modern Art. He received his B.A. in art and art education, with emphasis in sculpture, from the University of Northern Iowa in 1964. In 1973-74 he designed and installed the inaugural exhibition at the Hirshhorn Museum and Sculpture Garden in Washington, DC. Among antiquities shows he has designed were the "2000 Years of Nigerian Art" at the Detroit Institute of Arts and the "Treasures of Tutankhamun" for the Agyptisches Museum in West Berlin.

## William Kissiloff

President of Kissiloff Associates, Inc., a New York planning and design organization, Kissiloff is an industrial design graduate of Pratt Institute, and has worked as a designer of graphics programs, exhibitions, museums and visitor centers for a variety of corporations, institutions and government agencies in the U.S. and abroad. Corporate clients include Rockefeller Center, AT&T, the Bowery Savings Bank, Procter & Gamble and Amtrak. He has designed Expo pavilions and international expositions at Bucharest, Tokyo, Zagreb and Bangkok for the U.S. Government's International Communication Agency and Department of Agriculture. Museum Projects involved the National Science Foundation, the Hall of Science in New York and the National Baseball Hall of Fame.

## Arthur Rosenblatt

Since 1968, Arthur Rosenblatt, AIA, has been vice president, architecture and planning, of the Metropolitan Museum of Art in New York. Before that he served as first deputy administrator/commissioner of the City of New York's Parks, Recreation and Cultural Affairs Administration. Rosenblatt received a certificate in architecture from the Cooper Union and then went on to earn his Bachelor of Architecture from Carnegie Mellon University in 1956. He was president of the Architectural League of New York (1970-72) and a member of the board of directors of the New York Chapter of the American Institute of Architects (1967-68).

## Dorothy Twining Globus

Involved with museum work since her college days, as a summer intern at the Smithsonian Institution, Dorothy Twining Globus is currently coordinator of exhibitions for Cooper-Hewitt, the Smithsonian's national museum of design in New York City. Globus interned at the Smithsonian for three summers beginning in 1966 while working toward her BA in art history at Swarthmore College. After graduation she returned to the Smithsonian full time as an exhibits researcher, coordinator and specialist. In 1973 she moved to New York to work on exhibitions at the Cooper-Hewitt, including "Man Transforms," the two-years-in-the-making show with which the museum reopened in 1976 under Smithsonian aegis in the former Andrew Carnegie mansion on upper Fifth Avenue.

## Laurent Marquart

Swiss-born Laurent Marquart is vice-president and director of Guillon, Smith, Marquart Associates Ltee of Montreal. The Canadian firm specializes in exhibition and museum design, environmental graphics and corporate identity programs. Marquart received a degree in graphic design from the Ecole des Arts Decoratifs in Geneva, Switzerland, in 1958. He worked as an illustrator and as a graphic, exhibit and showcase designer in Italy, England and Switzerland (in Lausanne on the National Swiss Exhibition, Expo 64) and taught art in Haiti before joining his present firm, then known as Jacques Guillon & Associates, in 1965 as graphic and exhibit designer, project director and assistant to the theme design coordinator for Expo 67.

## Casebook Writer

**Edward K. Carpenter**

A writer on various aspects of architecture and design, Carpenter has been an editor for architectural and design magazines and is the author of a number of books, including *Casebooks 2 and 3/Best in Exhibition Design*. His most recent book is *Design Review 25*.

## Index Exhibitions

## Clients/Sponsoring Organizations

## Design Firms/ Designers/Consultants

# Cape Building Services
# Boards and Panels

Working with an exhibit budget of slightly more than $60,000, Pentagram Design of London had four months to design and install a trade exhibit for the National Building Exhibition in Birmingham, England. Covering 2000 sq. ft. with a stand which displayed the client's (Cape Building Services') products (insulation, column casings, wall and ceiling panels, etc.) being installed and used, their solution is bold and direct. "To the point," the Casebook jurors called it. Pentagram painted the parts of its stand which weren't white, blue, "because we liked it," says designer John McConnell. In keeping with the no-nonsense approach, they used stencils for lettering. Forms within the stand included slanting roofs (displaying roof panels), curving pipes covered with Cape insulation, and simulated I-shaped girders protected by Cape column casings. Overhead hung a space frame with yellow canvas sections proclaiming "Cape." The stand was voted best in show.

1. Bird's-eye drawing of Cape Industries Ltd.'s 2000-sq. ft. installation at Great Britain's National Building Exhibition.
2. Graphics are stenciled on fabric stretched from pipe frameworks beneath open-truss ceiling.
3, 4. Products (insulation and column casings) are displayed in simulated building situations.

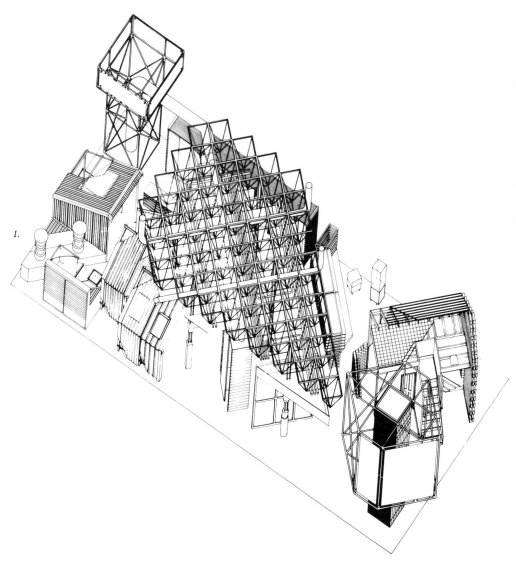

1.

2.

3.

4.

**11/Exhibition Design**

5.

5. Slanting cut-away roof panels harbor
   exhibit visitors.
6. Phantom, cut-out workman installs
   Cape insulation.

**Client:** Cape Building Services
Ltd. (Uxbridge, England)
**Design firm:** Pentagram Design,
London
**Designers:** Ron Herran, John
McConnell, David Pearce, Tom
Politowicz
**Fabricator:** Beck & Pollitzer
Contracts Ltd.

6.

# Africa in Antiquity: The Arts of Ancient Nubia and the Sudan

Originating at the Brooklyn Museum, the "Africa in Antiquity" exhibit was designed both to travel and to fit the space allotted it in Brooklyn. Fitting the space was a problem because the space was huge—12,000 sq. ft. of the third floor Great Hall Ambulatory, whose ceiling arches peaked at 28 ft.—and the objects displayed were mostly small. The artifacts, dug up as a result of the building of Egypt's Aswan Dam, included pieces of gold jewelry, pottery, sandstone statues and busts, the smallest a few centimeters across, the largest (a city of Faras fresco) 7' tall and 3' wide.

Designer Charles B. Froom had the task of making visitors forget the vast space and pay attention to the artifacts, and he did this in two ways. First, he created a framework of sheetrock walls from 12' to 16' high within the Ambulatory's walls, and within that he had built what he calls a secondary structure of walls 12' high and varying thicknesses tied together by massive sheetrock lintels, which held electrical wiring. Into this secondary structure fit the display cases (and their lighting), which housed the show's objects and which traveled to other museums. (The secondary structure traveled mostly as schematic drawings.) These cases were about 3½', 6' or 8' long and were obviously more humanly scaled than the lofty Ambulatory. But Froom used still another method to scale down the space and pinpoint visitors' attention. His second method was color. The ceiling in the Ambulatory is blue and though he couldn't change it (the cost of a scaffolding alone made ceiling painting prohibitive), he

painted his sheetrock walls white, used softer colors on his secondary structure, off-whites and beige, then within the cases themselves used darker hues, gray-greens and browns, for instance.

Further, within each case he gave each artifact identity by mounting it individually, either against its own relief pilaster or on its own stand, elevating each item to adult eye-level. Larger objects sat directly on the case's floor. Cups or bowls that one might want to see into were mounted close to the floor and tilted slightly forward.

Low-wattage bulbs, floods and spots, picked out individual artifacts or washed the case. These lights went in an attic attached to the top of each case, in an area equal to the case itself and separated from it by a three-layered panel. This panel consisted of a ⅛" layer of plexiglass, a #30 stainless steel wire cloth and a ⅛" layer of Sanapex glass, which has a slight obscuring tendency, interrupting a direct view of the lighting apparatus but allowing a spotlight shining through to pick out small objects. The plexiglass layer kept glass from falling into the case should the glass break.

Wall panels in Helvetica type introduced the show, explained the region's geography, the people who live there and their art. And the show ended with a section on contemporary Nubia, whose people still speak the ancient language and in many instances use the ancient art motifs in their household items. Some of these appeared in a continuous 12-minute slide show.

In between were artifacts from five different historical

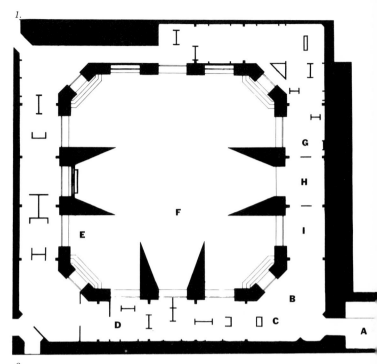

Key to Plan:
A. Exhibition Entrance
B. Introductory Gallery
C. Complete New Enclosure Around Entire Ambulatory Galleries
D. Case Support Enclosures
E. Scrim Panels
F. Center Court
G. Exhibition Conclusion
H. Ancillary Gallery Exhibition
I. Audio-Visual Unit

1. *Plan.*
2. *Sheetrock structure scales down huge Brooklyn Museum space for display of small objects.*

All photographs courtesy Department of Egyptian and Classical Art, The Brooklyn Museum.

3.

4.

5.

6.

eras, arranged chronologically. Between each era's space were wall plaques (in Helvetica) explaining what one had just seen and announcing something of what came next.

Froom, taking his schematic drawings, went with the exhibit to Seattle and New Orleans, where he helped set it up in its new spaces.

**Client:** Brooklyn Museum, New York City; Floyd Lattin, exhibitions coordinator
**Design firm:** Charles B. Froom/ Design, Brooklyn, New York
**Designer:** Charles B. Froom
**Curator:** Bernard Bothmer, curator of Egyptology, Brooklyn Museum
**Fabricator:** Designgroup, Inc., Jerome Lawton, president

3-5. *Each artifact is individually mounted in its own case, on its own pedestal, or against its own pilaster, and each item is individually lighted.*
6. *Lighting is in sheetrock attics above each case.*
7. *Sheetrock substructure even has its own doorways scaled down to suit the small artifacts beneath a 28' ceiling.*

7.

# Brooklyn Children's Museum

In the heart of Brooklyn is a museum whose exhibits may influence profoundly the future of exhibit design. Though the exhibits are aimed mostly at children, roughly from five to 12 years, there is no reason why these or similar exhibits cannot appeal to older children or even adults. Indeed, there is reason to believe that children can learn the most from these exhibits when guided gently by an adult.

Learning is the fundamental concept behind the exhibits, which were designed according to an exhibit concept developed by Dr. Edwin Schlossberg when he was the museum's administrator of exhibit design. According to some educational theorists, children from ages five to 12 learn best by manipulating things around them, by taking hold of things and using them, and this is the theory the Brooklyn Children's Museum's exhibits put into practice.

The exhibits are designed so that children will touch and do things with them, having a lot of fun and learning a lot all at once, and the designers at Saville Design in New York who designed the exhibit devices tried to make it obvious what children should do with each object and display. This aim was only partially successful; and though the museum staff has partly overcome the problem by adding captions and brief written directions to some displays, the Saville designers think both displays and children would be better served if adults could lead children through the museum suggesting things to be done. To this end, Brent Saville proposes a guidance manual, which would help teachers, parents, and museum staffers use the exhibits

1.

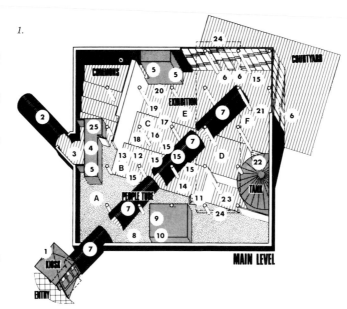

MAIN LEVEL

1. Main Entrance (1907 Trolley Car Kiosk).
2. Delivery Tube (Service Entrance).
3. Service Area.
4. Service Elevator.
5. Stairways (to all levels).
6. Exits to Courtyard.
7. People Tube/Neon Helix/Stream.
8. Reception Area/Checkroom.
9, 10. Restrooms.
11. Steps to Mezzanine (Staff Offices/Research Library).
12. Ripple Tank.
13. Movable Freezer Unit.
14. Steam Engine.
15. Curved Space Labyrinths.
16. Calliope.
17. Windmill.
18. Compressed-Air Lift.
19. Counterbalance Lift.
20. Collections Cupboard.
21. Greenhouse.
22. Tank (Auditorium).
23. Marketplace (Retail Shop).
24. Staff Mezzanine (dotted lines).
25. Staff Pantry-Kitchen.

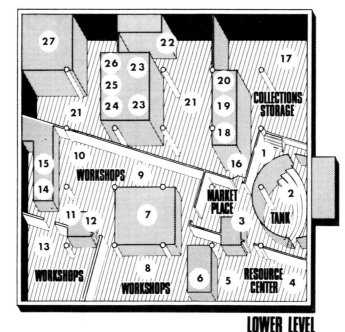

LOWER LEVEL

1. Steps Leading Down from Greenhouse to Tank and Marketplace Areas.
2. Tank (Auditorium).
3. Marketplace (Retail Shop).
4. Children's Library.
5. Take-Home Collection.
6. Photography Workshop.
7. Offices and Workshops.
8. Science Workshop Area.
9. Teaching Materials Storage Area.
10. Arts and Crafts Workshop Area.
11, 12. Restrooms.
13. Dance Studio Workshop.
14. Stairway to Other Levels.
15. Service Elevator.
16. Steps Leading Down to Collection Maintenance Areas.
17. Collections Storage Area.
18. Office.
19. Graphics Room.
20. Office of Educational Program I for Collections.
21. Building Maintenance and Exhibit Preparation Areas.
22. Stairway Up to Other Levels.
23. Staff Locker Rooms.
24. Storage.
25. Mimeograph Room.
26. Office.
27. Boiler Room.

2.

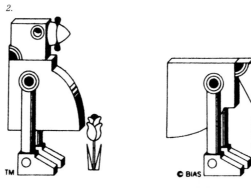

with the children. Saville sees a manual as a natural extension of the exhibits. "If a designer designs a product, he does a user's manual," says Saville. "Why shouldn't he do the same for a museum display?"

As it is, children who involve themselves with the exhibits become imaginatively absorbed in a way not conceivable with static exhibits, whose only nod to participation may be a button for someone to push. Though the Brooklyn Children's Museum is the first to focus entirely on exhibits meant to be played with, other museums throughout the country offer an occasional glimpse into this way of teaching. About a dozen U.S. museums offer a somewhat similar approach, in Fort Worth, Little Rock, Jacksonville, Boston, Indianapolis and elsewhere, and most of these museums aim their exhibits primarily at children.

These are some of the displays encased in the Brooklyn Children's Museum's new underground (to preserve a park above it) building, designed by Hardy Holzman Pfeiffer Associates:

• A greenhouse in which children can mix soil and gather seeds to grind into flour in a nearby grist mill.

• A bright red and yellow steam engine to which visitors can add water, watch steam run the engine and sound its whistle.

• A river of water running 180′ through the neon-ringed, corrugated sewer culverts that are the museum's main entranceway. This river, about three feet across and an inch or so deep, has a series of locks, dams, water wheels, a turbine and other devices that can be worked by visitors to make the

1. *Plan.*
2. *Museum symbol appears on promotional material.*
3. *Children climb on plastic model of a diamond crystal molecule.*
4. *Water-trough river runs through entrance way beneath corrugated sewer culvert.*

4.

water level rise or fall and its velocity speed up or slow down. (It runs downhill, drains out at the end and is pumped back to the start. Should the water level get too high or too low, the pump shuts off automatically.) The museum maintains a fleet of small wooden boats for people to play with in the water.

• A farm windmill from Beatrice, Nebraska, which visitors can make whirl and twist to face the wind from two ceiling fans. Below the windmill is a bright red pump whose pipe is cut away and encased in plexiglass to expose its piston as, driven by the wind, it pumps water into a trough. If the windmill is detached, visitors can work the pump by hand.

• A 1920s air-driven calliope made by the Tangley Company in Muscatine, Iowa.

• Two giant, clear, curved space structures, models of a protein and a diamond crystal molecule, models built to a scale of eight billion to one; a small child climbing within them is in scale with the size of an atom.

In all, the museum has some 40,000 artifacts, collected since it first opened, in the same Brooklyn park, in 1899. About 500 to 1000 of these are on display in a plexiglass-fronted cupboard. Visitors can borrow many of the smaller ones for up to two weeks, and there is a brisk traffic in small, durable African sculpture and musical instruments such as rattles, gourds, drums, and whistles.

One enters Hardy Holzman Pfeiffer's underground museum building through a 1907 copper-roofed trolley kiosk (which leads to the sewer conduit). Inside is a large, open-plan space (30,000 sq. ft.) on four levels, each four feet below the former. Saville

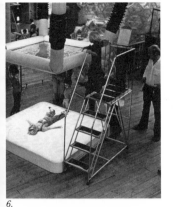

6.

7.

8.

Design designed devices to carry passengers from level to level and involve them with the movement. An air lift, which can be pumped by hand or by pushing a button, has a platform on top of a bellows. A counter-balance lift works like a seesaw; and an open hydraulic lift works like a car lift in a filling station.

Brent Saville thinks that, with proper coaching, teachers and museum attendants could get children involved in the exhibits in special ways, helping them understand whole sequences of natural events. One could, for instance, grow grain in the green house, reap the seeds, grind them into flour, bake the flour into bread and eat it. There are innumerable uses to which the exhibits can be put with proper imagination and incentive. Small children may learn best by doing, but someone still has to show them what to do.

9.

10.

11.

5-10. Museum is filled with items children (and their parents) can touch, manipulate, fondle, stroke, play with, use, and learn from.
11, 12. Promotional brochure describes museum's history and purpose.

**Client:** Brooklyn Children's Museum, a department of the Brooklyn Institute of Arts and Science
**Design firm:** Saville Design, New York City; Brooklyn Children's Museum
**Designers:** Dr. Edwin Schlossberg (concept), Brent Saville, Leonard Berta, Kenneth B. Smith
**Consultant:** Synestructics, Inc., Peter Pearce, president (curved space structures)
**Fabricator:** Saville Design

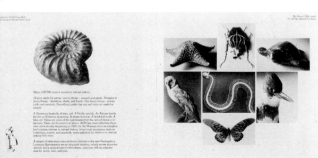

12.

## New York Times Ad Expo Exhibit

A month before the Ad Expo advertising conference opened in New York City's Coliseum, The New York Times advertising director told the newspaper's promotion department he'd taken space for an exhibit. For a while the Times' management thought an old portable exhibit lurked somewhere in the Times building on West 43rd Street, waiting like a tired warrior for new action, but no one ever found it. So the promotion department designed one, making it portable, to be stored and used again. Working with a $30,000 budget, the designers hinged together large pieces of plywood, 9' high and 3' wide,

covered them with paper-thin coatings of stainless steel, and on these coatings silk-screened photos and text from the newspaper, creating montages.

The space the Times took was 20' by 40', and within it they arranged the exhibit in five areas around a central space filled with small cube tables and canvas chairs where salesmen could sit and talk to customers.

Each exhibit area portrayed one of the new sections the Times had recently added to its weekday and Sunday editions, such as "Home" and "Entertainment." And a special exhibit area held photos of the Times' 45 Pulitzer Prize-

winners, with explanations of what the awards were for. Introducing each area was a New York Times logo, silk-screened vertically onto one of the hinged panels, rising 9' high so that, as one entered the exhibit, one saw five repetitions of this giant logo. Panels hinged in groups of five could be arranged to undulate like a Chinese screen or grouped to form a pentagonal column. Also part of the exhibit was a counter (constructed of plywood and stainless steel coating) which held promotional material, brochures and rate sheets.

To move the exhibit workmen merely fold up the panels, like Arabs striking tents, and carry

them swiftly away.

What was the most satisfying aspect of the assignment? Because of the compressed time, there would be no second guessing, and everything moved quickly. "This was one of those jobs that go smoothly with no problems at any point," noted designer Paul F. Kutil. And then, as if knocking on wood, he added: "That doesn't happen too often."

The Casebook jurors thought the exhibit "clever" and "bright."

1.

1. *Hinged plywood panels undulate to enclose space at Ad Expo conference.*
2. *One section of New York Times exhibit was filled with photos of the paper's 45 Pulitzer Prize-winners.*
3. *Collages of the newspaper's format were silk-screened on stainless steel coatings given the plywood panels.*

**Client:** The New York Times
**Design firm:** Promotion Department, The New York Times
**Designers:** Paul F. Kutil; Andrew Kner, art director; Joseph Mazzocchi, production.
**Fabricator:** Deluca LaCapra Exhibits, Inc.

2.

3.

# Hall of American
# Maritime Enterprise

Key:
1. Fresnel Lens (3½ Order)
2. Colonial Warehouse
3. Ship *Brilliant*
4. *Brilliant* Foremast
5. Whaleboat
6. Stevens Engine
7. *J.M. White*
8. Pilothouse
9. Lock, Pool, and Dam Model
10. Fresnel Lens (3rd Order)
11. Bell Buoy
12. Francis Life Car
13. Underwriters' Office
14. *Oak* Engine
15. Sperry Gyropilot
16. Sickels Steering Gear
17. *Majestic* Skylight
18. *Leviathan* Room
19. Tattoo Parlor
20. Scrimshaw

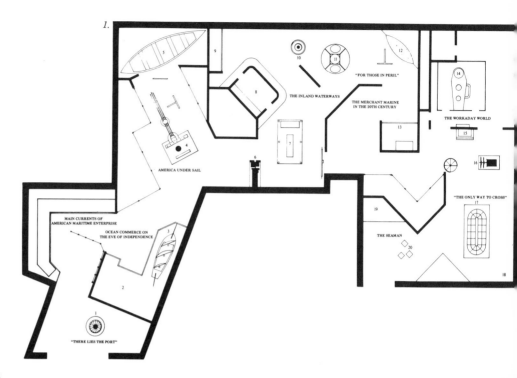

For more than a year, curators and designers in the Smithsonian Institution's National Museum of History & Technology struggled with the seemingly insurmountable problem of arrangement. A Hall of American Maritime Enterprise had long been a dream of the museum's maritime curator, Dr. Melvin H. Jackson (now retired), and for ten years he had been soliciting sponsorship and collecting items for display. Some of these items were huge. The complete working engine room of the U.S. Coast Guard buoy tender *Oak* took up space, as did its deck house and the complete pilothouse of a contemporary Mississippi River towboat.

Both curators and designers hoped to arrange the material chronologically, starting 200 years ago with colonial shipping and working down to the 1970s.

2.

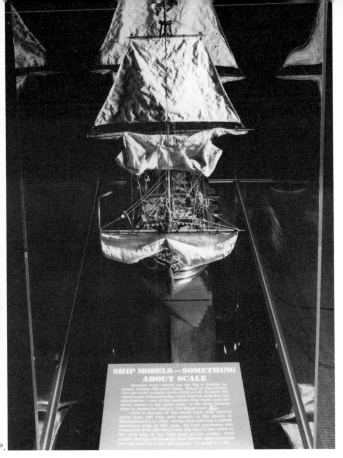

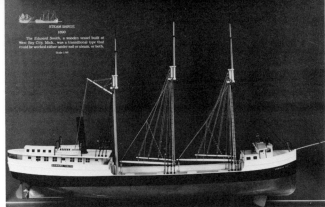

4.

5.

But most of the large items, such as the *Oak*'s engine (which runs on compressed air), a bell buoy and a couple of lighthouse lenses, lights and rotating mechanisms came from the 20th century. Any chronological arrangement left a mass of heavy, bulky items at one end of the exhibit space. Fortunately, a scale model based on a script prepared by curator Dr. Robert C. Post made two things apparent: that the hall would need more floor space than originally allocated and that a chronological arrangement was not going to work. The latter problem was dealt with by switching to an episodic approach in which artifacts and models were arranged in sections devoted to, for example, ocean trade, inland shipping, luxury liners, and a sailor's life, and the problem of insufficient space was solved by adding to the hall's

proposed floor space — on the first floor of the National Museum of History and Technology — with space taken from adjacent agricultural and automotive exhibits. But even with 14,000 sq. ft. of floor space they had more material than they could comfortably fit in. There are more than 100 ship models, for instance, the largest a 13′ model of the 1775 three-masted schooner *Brilliant,* one-tenth the ship's original size. (A full-scale replica of its foremast is installed later on in the exhibit.) There are four full-scale, fully-furnished period rooms: a tattoo parlor, a radio shack, a tobacco warehouse, and a marine insurance underwriter's office. In the tattoo parlor, a hidden projector projects tattoos of eagles and hearts onto a mannikin of a young sailor. Another particularly effective

use of film is in the pilot house of the Mississippi towboat, through whose front window you watch a film of the passing Mississippi, narrated by a contemporary river pilot.

Elsewhere throughout the exhibit, four slide shows display photos of four major U.S. ports as they were at various times in the last 200 years and as they are now. Chanties play in the background in the Sailor's Life section and in the Whaling section. Also at spots in the exhibit are huge photomurals produced by 3M's photoscan technique. These panoramas, 14′ high and 30′ long, show a New England whaling scene, World War II Victory ships coming off an assembly line, Pittsburgh inland waterway paddlewheelers lined up, and the *Mark Hassel* burning.

Perhaps the exhibit's most

popular section is the For-Those-in-Peril area, where lightographs show storms and disasters at sea amidst the reproduction of newspaper accounts, flares, life jackets, life boats and a lighted Coast Guard bell buoy. Also here is a film composed of clips from Hollywood sea films: Spencer Tracy facing a storm; Barbara Stanwyck watching the *Titanic* sink; Gregory Peck harpooning Moby Dick.

Helping tie everything together is a timeline. Its framework, like all the exhibit's cases and frames, is of white pine. Its surface is plexiglass slanted at a 30-degree angle. Nine color lines silk-screened on the back of the plexiglass correspond to sections of the exhibit. And photos dropped into position in these colored bands tell the chronological story.

6.

7.

8.

Above the timeline hang additional photos. Captions are in stencil type because stencil was and still is the typeface used on most shipping notes.

Because so many models appear, the designers placed a silhouette of the *Mayflower* next to the silhouette of every model to give an idea of scale.

The million-dollar budget was used to purchase some of the larger items, to demolish the adjacent space, to construct cases and frameworks, to produce graphics and to pay salaries of temporary assistants. The floor has a Jack Lenor Larsen sisal carpet.

While the Casebook jurors grumbled somewhat about the use of "too much" wood, they liked the way the designers had used the space, covering every surface. "A massive assault," the jurors called it.

9.

10.

6-8. *Walls have layered look, with cases and panels hung over photomural. Circular stairs (Fig. 8, lower right) lead to engine room of Coast Guard buoy tender.*

9-11. *The 14,000-sq ft. exhibit space is packed with artifacts and photos. Sea chanties play in one section; in another film clips of Hollywood sea disasters are shown.*

11.

12.

13.

14.

12, 13. *Paddlewheeler models, photos and artifacts.*
14. *Mast and rigging replica of 18th-century schooner* Brilliant.
15. *Motion picture camera projects tattoos onto tattoo parlor mannikin.*

**Client:** National Museum of History and Technology, Smithsonian Institution (Washington, D.C.)
**Design firm:** Exhibits Design Office, National Museum of History and Technology
**Designers:** Nadya Makovenyi; Claudine Klose, assistant
**Consultants:** Dr. Robert C. Post, curator, historian; Elso M. Burton; Peggy L. Sawyer; Dr. Robert D. Friedel; Francis D. Roche, collections manager; Charles H. Rowell, period rooms; Benjamin W. Lawless, audio-visual; John N. Stine, head of major object restoration and installation
**Fabricator:** Walter Lewis, chief, exhibits production, National Museum of History and Technology

15.

# Subways

Developing a traveling exhibit to be set up in subway stations posed problems that, if not special, were at least extraordinary. How could the exhibit be protected from vandalism? And from graffiti artists? How could it be designed to be set up and dismantled by unskilled workmen?

Originally designed for the Cooper-Hewitt Museum as part of a series of exhibits on Immovable Objects, with a grant from the National Endowment for the Arts, and now traveling to ten subway stations in ten U.S. and Canadian cities under the Smithsonian Institution's sponsorship, the exhibit had, as it turned out, its subject matter to protect it. The subject was subways. And Samuel Lebowitz Design designed it so it can be taken in on the move, as people rush past it to catch a train. It also invites more contemplative examination. Evidently its message—that subways can be clean, attractive, pleasant places to be—has at least impressed subway riders enough so far to keep the exhibit free of graffiti or other vandalism.

But Sam Lebowitz took no chances with the design. He made it sturdy. The framework is a heavy architectural steel Unistrut system, and the panels which hold the exhibit's graphics are masonite over a paper honeycomb core. Mounted on these panels with pressure-sensitive adhesive, the graphics are then covered by ⅛" acrylic held in place by an aluminum frame. Lebowitz designed a fitting to hold the panels within the Unistrut system. This fitting is merely a simple bracket that can be tightened and loosened by a workman with a socket wrench. In all, the exhibit has 13 display modules, each 7′ high, 7′ long and 4′ deep that can be strung together forming a 91′ surface—182′ if you count both sides. Each module contains overhead fluorescent lighting with wiring set up so each panel can be plugged separately into an electrical source or connected to its neighbors, allowing one electrical socket to feed power to the entire exhibit.

Lebowitz used a headline and photograph format to get across his points. For instance, the text "Platforms near street level, station maps that illuminate the route and frequent stops make the Metro—and all corners of Paris—easily accessible, even to visitors" goes with color photos of Paris Metro kiosks and stations.

The exhibit treats 11 subways in detail and mentions others. (The 11 are: Paris, London, Stockholm, Tokyo, Moscow, Montreal, BART, Washington, D.C., New York, Baltimore and Boston.) Besides 350 color and black-and-white photos, the exhibit displays system maps, drawings, cartoons and posters. Much of this material could not be altered in size, and its arrangement called for what Lebowitz terms "a highly disciplined geometry." Essentially what he did was arrange the graphics against bands of gray, white and black backing running the length of the exhibit like subway trains. It took 10 months to put the exhibit together on a $75,000 budget.

To go with each installation, the Cooper-Hewitt Museum printed a tabloid newspaper catalogue, which it sells for a dollar at newsstands in each city the exhibit visits.

*1. Exhibit poster.*

**Client:** Cooper-Hewitt Museum (New York), Smithsonian Institution
**Design firm:** Samuel Lebowitz Design, New York
**Fabricators:** Cooper-Hewitt Museum staff; Globe Strut, U.S. Gypsum Corp. (structural system); Stuart M. Penny Labs (custom photo prints); Foto-Ready Production (typography); S.D. Scott Co. (catalogue printing)

2.

5.

3.

6.

4.

7.

2-4. Tabloid newspaper catalogue is sold at newsstands in cities visited by subway exhibit.
5-8. Modular Unistrut system holds panels with advertising-like graphics (maps, cartoons, drawings and photos with headlines and minimal text).

# Exhibition Design/28

## Our Fourth Show: Dabbling and Fooling Around

The exuberance of Southern Illinois University's student design show is evident in its title. This exuberance, along with ingenuity, hard work and a certain bravado made up for a lack of money. It had to, for as work got under way the student design organization, Design Initiative, whose 23 members guided the show's design, had only $800 in its till, $400 of which represented a donation from student government. Scrounging, fortunately, is a highly developed art form among students and soldiers, and the students combined strategic borrowing with gracious acceptance of donated materials to assemble a framework on which to hang their show. Construction scaffolding and spotlights came from campus departments; large cardboard panels (44″ by 108″ and 81″ by 108″) came free from International Paper Company. Using fiberglass tape slung over the scaffolding's pipes and fastened to the cardboard panels with nylon machine bolts, the students hung the cardboard panels as graphic display surfaces. Cardboard podiums and shelves became display surfaces for three-dimensional student designs — games, furniture, electronic gear, etc. At one position within the maze of scaffolding, a three-screen slide show displayed still more student work.

Arranging the 10′-high scaffolding sections into corridors and enclosures, the students grouped their work in four categories: computer-aided design, product design, urban design and visual communications. Displayed were posters, brochures, packaging, photos and drawings, as well as three-dimensional items such as an alarm box that can be used by an immobilized patient in a wheel chair to call for help. The show had, in spots, a hectic flea-market look, but if its appearance was informal, it was also occasionally elegant; and the students chose a Korinna typeface for captions and invitations because they felt a sophisticated typeface would enhance the show's formality.

In the windows of Quigley Hall, whose 60′-by-40′ lounge housed the show, students set up displays promoting the show inside. Perhaps the best of these window displays was a three-dimensional cardboard cutout of a silhouette presented by design students posing enthusiastically for a group photo.

Banners of borrowed canvas proclaimed the show, too, hanging outside and inside Quigley Hall. All graphics on the banners were applique, formed by hot-gluing canvas graphics to the canvas banners.

The whole show was set up in 28 hours, from 3 p.m. on a Saturday to 7 p.m. on Sunday.

The Casebook jurors liked what they called the show's "approach." The students found most stimulating the help they got from other campus departments and the enthusiastic attendance. As a result of the show, they report, some students at Southern Illinois changed their majors to design.

**Client:** Design Department, Southern Illinois University (Carbondale)
**Design firm:** Design Initiative, student design organization
**Designers:** Steve Bennett, Pat Haney, Tony Lee, Scott Linde, Karl Schurtz, Warren Williamson
**Advisor:** Thomas Kachel

1.

2.

Dabbling and Fooling Around

3.

4.

5.

6.

7.

8.

1. Banner proclaims student design
   show at Southern Illinois University.
2. Students are part of the design.
3-7. Cardboard panels hung on
   scrounged construction scaffolding
   are background for graphics.
   Three-dimensional designs are
   displayed on cardboard podiums and
   shelves.
8. Window display in window of
   building housing student exhibit is a
   microcosm of the exhibit within.

# Feather Arts

Phyllis Rabineau had the idea. It started as a private fantasy, she says. And when she took it public, it caught the fancy of a lot of other people at Chicago's Field Museum of Natural History, where she is a curator in the anthropology department. What Rabineau envisioned was an exhibit of featherwork, of *all* the featherwork stored in the museum's collections: jewelry and baskets inlaid with feathers, feathers woven to form headdresses, shawls and blankets, feathers once used as money or to give their wearer the courage of a bird of prey.

She had a lot of enthusiastic help in going through the museum's storage rooms looking for feathered items, cleaning and restoring them and arranging them in a traveling exhibit, scheduled to appear in California, New York and Pennsylvania before returning to Chicago. For instance, Shauna Clark did the restoration, repairing damage and bringing faded colors back to life. Ron Testa took catalogue photos that show the feathers' textures and moods. Exhibit designer Clifford Abrams helped choose the items for display and worked at most everything else in the four months it took to put the exhibit together. Besides the usual design of the exhibit and its lighting, he handled all correspondence, photo research, design of supplementary graphics such as posters, flyers, brochures, the 90-page catalogue, invitations, etc. He also did the graphic production and supervised the exhibit's production and installation.

The exhibit has four sections, showing feather work from various cultures in all parts of the world pertaining to beauty

(ornamental nose feathers, for example), wealth (feather money), spirit (shield covers, sorcerers' shoes, etc.) and a section on how to feather. Announced by overhead red cloth banners, each section has some nine cases, usually grouped together, which Abrams borrowed from other sections of the museum. These cases are made from an Abstracta framework with Masonite panels enclosing their top and bottom sections the way cloth or paper encloses the ends of a box kite. Featherwork is displayed in a 4' by 4' by 4' midsection, which starts either two or four feet off the floor and is enclosed in plexiglass on three sides. This midsection's fourth side is usually a masonite panel, either painted brown or holding a photo blowup against which artifacts are displayed.

Within the cases Abrams positioned the feathered artifacts to "fill the space." Some he hung from the cases' plexiglass tops by drilling holes in them, passing rods fastened to monofilament lines through the holes and tying feathered artifacts to the end of the lines. Some items he raised off the case's floor on plexiglass stands, which he fashioned especially for certain pieces. Next to each object he silk-screened captions in Palatino type, chosen because it offers a complete family of legible type.

Lighting posed a special problem. Feathers' organic coloring is sensitive to intense light and heat, so to prevent damage to the artifacts, Abrams designed a 5.5-volt lighting system, which travels with the cases wherever they go. What he did was modify a track lighting system, suspending it within the Abstracta system above each

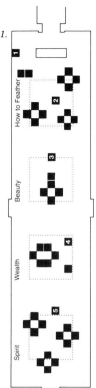

1.

2.

3.

case's midsection, letting light shine through a top plexiglass panel above the display.

Positioning items within the cases was the crux of the exhibit, and Abrams spent a good deal of time working out the arrangement of items for each case. Surrounding himself with all 260 specimens to be mounted in the show, Abrams worked case by case. But instead of filling all the cases, he worked initially with only one, positioning items in it carefully, marking where to drill holes for monofilament lines. Sometimes as many as 15 items fitted into a case, and Abrams took almost a full day arranging them. Sometimes a case with only two items would take no more than a few minutes. Once an arrangement was established, Abrams took a Polaroid photograph of it, then removed

the items and started over, arranging new items in the same case. Finally, cases were set up in the exhibit space and their contents arranged from the photographs.

Abrams' concern was with filling the space esthetically. He wanted each piece of featherwork to be visible from at least three sides, and he wanted spaces between objects to be natural and uncluttered, so he considered with extra care the space around each item. Other than that, he says he did nothing special. Where possible, he raised small items to eye level. Big items went toward the back of each case. When there's a photo in a case, it shows one of the displayed items in use—a headdress being worn, for instance, or men negotiating with feather money.

. *Floor plan. Broken lines indicate
hanging banners; numbered boxes are
label stands. Note cruciform grouping of
cases.*

*, 4. Exhibit logo.*

*, 5-7. Artifacts are arranged to fill
space within cases three-
dimensionally. Some items are hung
from top of cases on monofilament
lines, some mounted on plexiglass
stands. One wall of some cases holds
a photo blowup of feather items in
use.*

**Client:** Field Museum of Natural
History (Chicago)
**Design firm:** Exhibition Department,
Field Museum
**Designers:** Clifford Abrams, project
director; Don Emery, design assistant.
**Curator:** Phyllis Rabineau, Department
of Anthropology
**Fabricators:** Exhibition Department,
Field Museum; Daniel Weinstock,
Christine Ingraham, lead preparators;
Al Schiske, head preparator

# Treasures from the Kremlin

By the time Lucian J. Leone got back from Russia, he had only three and a half months until the exhibit was to open at New York's Metropolitan Museum of Art. He'd gone to Moscow to look at—in their natural setting in the Kremlin—the 100 or so artifacts for which he was to design a setting in New York. Some of these artifacts were religious: icons, crosses, chalices, etc. Some were secular: arms and armor, embroideries and items used in the coronation of the czars— historical objects dating from the 12th to the 20th century. They had never been out of Russia before. And Leone, realizing that Russia, Moscow, and more particularly, the architecture of the Kremlin, said a great deal about their design, came back with a lot of photographs, which, blown up, form the initial part of the Metropolitan's exhibit, "Treasures from the Kremlin," setting the mood for what follows.

Leone divided the exhibit into three sections, giving each a distinct color, green, gold, and red, colors found on the dome of St. Basil's, one of the Kremlin churches. The show's first section was a 24' wide, 137' long introductory gallery, whose green walls were lined with Leone's enlarged, stunning photographs of the Kremlin's buildings. Next came a gold walled gallery, 24' by 30', in which the show really started. Here, centered on a pedestal in its own vitrine, was the 12th-century silver-gilt chalice that belonged to Yuri Dolgorukiy, the prince who founded Moscow. On the walls hung icons, among them the 14th-century painted icon, "The Savior of the Fiery Eye." Next

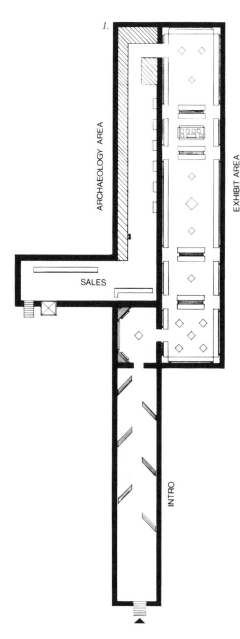

1. Floor plan.
2, 3. Many artifacts are in individual floor cases.

came the show's main section, a red-walled gallery, 200' long, divided into five sections in which the show's fabrics, paintings, silver, gold, jewel-crusted, plexiglass-encased artifacts stood. Leone had seen the red he used here not only on the dome of St. Basil's but also in the bedroom of the Czars within the old Kremlin. And lest the intensity of the red on the walls be changed by the exhibit lighting, lighting designer Lemar Terry used undiluted incandescent bulbs throughout. At the end of the show was a corridor gallery of archeological finds within and beneath the Kremlin, bits of glass, bracelets, tile and earthenware, and stone and terracotta architectural details from 16th- and 17th-century Kremlin buildings.

Since so many of the show's artifacts were religious, Leone wanted to give them a complementary setting, and he accordingly designed a wall panel system which started 1' off the floor and 1' from the gallery walls, rising straight for 13', then canting out at a 45-degree angle for another 4'. This gave the space a vaguely cathedral-like feeling. Moreover, all the construction was needed, Leone maintains, because the space he was working with was vast, approximately 14,000 square feet, and the objects displayed mostly small. He couldn't let them get lost in a space that seemed over-large.

To go with these wall panels, Leone designed two basic modular cases, one to be mounted on the walls, one 7' 2" high with a square plan to stand on the floor. Using this modular approach, Leone kept the show's complexity from outrunning the $225,000 budget.

And because time was tight, too, Leone avoided a full-scale mockup, working only from a small space model.

All labels and copy were in the Kabel family of typefaces; the logo was in Rustikalis.

Though Leone took great pleasure in the exhibit's design, he values more the friendships he formed with the exhibit's Russian representatives. His enthusiasm for the project and the pleasure he took in the work, he says, stemmed from these friendships.

A grant from the Robert Wood Johnson, Jr., Charitable Trust made "Treasures from the Kremlin" possible.

**Client:** Metropolitan Museum of Art (New York)
**Design firm:** Design Department, Metropolitan Museum of Art
**Designer:** Lucian J. Leone
**Curator:** Curatorial staff, Metropolitan Museum of Art; Olga Raggio, curator in charge of "Treasures from the Kremlin"
**Consultant:** Lemar Terry, lighting
**Fabricator:** Building Department, Metropolitan Museum of Art

4. Blown-up color photos of Moscow stand at beginning of exhibit, setting the mood. Note potted birch trees meant to help with mood and break up space.
5. Photomural of Kremlin surrounds passage into main exhibit area.
6. Wall panels and wall cases are set against red walls.

# The Money Center

1. At exhibit entrance automated-
   mannikin teller invites you to open an
   account.
2. Philosophers' park explains economic
   theories of history's leading
   economists.

1.

A park fence with smiling knobs topping its waist-high metal spikes, a plate-glass shop window, and a metal framework with overhead banners are some of the devices with which the Burdick Group divides "The Money Center," an exhibit it designed for Chicago's Continental Illinois National Bank and Trust Co. at the Museum of Science and Industry. It is a permanent exhibit costing $1.5 million and it explains what money is and does by using some economic models that never saw the inside of a university classroom. "There were no precedents for attacking the study of economics three-dimensionally," says Bruce Burdick. Indeed, economics is not a subject that would draw exhibit crowds (the bank and the designers decided), but money is. Never mind that a study of money is part of economics.

The arcade of games, computerized tests of skill and ingenuity, puppet shows and pinball machines set up on 4500 sq. ft. of the museum's hardwood floors seems more like an amusement park than a place where you can learn something about how money works. And the crowds love it. It has been packed day after day since it opened. Not only do people flock to "The Money Center," but they also stick around for more than a fleeting glimpse. Visitors spend between 20 minutes and an hour and a half with the exhibit, reports the bank, and the main reason why is the computer.

Computer terminals are set up at the exhibit entrance and next to three-dimensional exhibits throughout the space. Twelve-digit keyboards and adjoining readout screens are linked to the Digital Equipment Company's PDP 1170 computer at the back of the exhibit.

Burdick thinks of his exhibit as a teaching machine. As you enter, an automated teller mannikin invites you to open an account, which you can do by getting an account number from the computer. Then, moving through the exhibit, you use the money in your account, spending it to increase your fortune or your wisdom, competing against the best players of that day, whose scores the computer flashes on its screens.

Standing next to an automated puppet show which has just performed a lesson in supply and demand using doughnuts and bakeries as examples, you are asked by the computer to run the doughnut business, budgeting advertising and materials and setting prices. The computer tells you how many you can sell on any given day at your prices. You bet the money in your account against your business ability, and you have as a goal the best score of the day. On one day, shortly after the exhibit opened, a reporter ran his $1000 up to $1135. High for the day was $286,574.

Past the entrance, where wood and glass display cases hold examples of items and symbols used as money since it was invented, are three steel pavilions:

Beneath the first pavilion the computer and an automated puppet show illustrate such abstractions as supply and demand and purchasing power and pricing.

The second pavilion, the philosophers' park, holds machines looking like tall, pedestal-mounted newspaper vending machines with

2.

newspaper-like displays that explain the theories of history's leading economists: Adam Smith, Thomas Malthus, David Ricardo, John Stuart Mill, Karl Marx and John Maynard Keynes. Included, too, are synopses of the lives and contributions of 20th-century Nobel laureates in economics.

The third pavilion illustrates where a consumer's money goes and how the money spreads through the economy, providing employment and income for others. Cash registers with multiple drawers hold models of items that consumers, businesses and government spend money on. Here, too, pinball machines illustrate the multiplier effect of a purchase. As long as you keep the ball in play, the machine and the economy store up points. When you stop, by taking your money and your ball out of play, the economy suffers.

By teaching easily grasped economic concepts in a way that is fun, the Continental Bank feels it can make everyone who sees the exhibit more knowledgeable about money and more receptive to the bank. The bank plans a series of workbook lessons that can be given to schoolchildren before they visit "The Money Center" and a final lesson they can take after their visit to gauge how much they've learned; and there is talk of possibly placing computer terminals in classrooms throughout the city, connected to the exhibit's computer. Moreover, the bank is planning a mini-Money Center in its lobby, with computer terminals linked to the main exhibit at the Museum of Science and Industry.

Eighteen months before the exhibit opened, the Continental Bank asked the Burdick Group if they could produce a money exhibit on a $500,000 budget. Outlining what they thought such an exhibit should be, the Burdick Group said they could do a better job for $1,500,000 and the bank went along. Judging from the exhibit and the reaction to it, everyone's getting his money's worth.

*3, 4. Computer terminals are spotted through exhibit. Visitors are asked to invest their account money according to economic principals explained in exhibit.*
*5. Pinball machine illustrates the multiplier effect of money spent.*
*6. Clear balls moving through plexiglass tubes help illustrate purchasing power.*
*7. Computer screen readouts.*
*8. Computer terminals are linked to computer at the back of the exhibit space.*
*9. Automated puppet show illustrates law of supply and demand.*

**Client:** Continental Illinois National Bank (Chicago)
**Design firm:** The Burdick Group, San Francisco
**Designers:** Bruce Burdick, Andrew Kramer, Stephen Hamilton
**Consultant:** Epstein & Berghorn, computer engineers
**Fabricator:** General Exhibits & Displays, Inc.

*3.*

*4.*

*5.*

8.

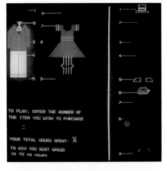

9.

# Ornament in the 20th Century

In 200 B.C., the Roman playwright Plautus had one of his characters observe that "A ship and a woman are never sufficiently adorned or too much." Though that thought may merely reflect one of Plautus's prejudices, ornamentation seems to be an innate human need, persisting throughout history despite temporary fads, trends, or philosophical arguments denying it.

One of the objectives of the Cooper-Hewitt Museum's exhibit, "Ornament in the 20th Century," was to document the important role ornament plays in contemporary design — or as a museum spokesman states: "to counter the notion that contemporary design is concerned only with minimalism and functionalism."

In all, the show, which ran for three months, held some 500

items: furniture, table place settings, jewelry, logos, billboards, posters and architecture (represented by photo blowups and by some of its elements: doors, windows, floors, walls, moldings, screens, railings and light fixtures).

But one entered the exhibit through the foyer of the former Andrew Carnegie House on New York's Fifth Avenue to confront just four items: a yellow Rolls Royce decorated with painted flowers and swirling garlands of leaves, a mock-up of one of the airplanes Alexander Calder decorated for Braniff Airlines, the poster of a woman painted from toe to hairline in honor of a New York Art Directors Club show, and a photo blowup of Watts Towers in Los Angeles. "We thought these things summed up 20th-century ornamentation," says one of the show's designers, Dorothy Twining Globus, and indeed they do. Calder's plane was suspended from the ceiling. The Rolls, a gift to the Cooper-Hewitt from John Lennon and Yoko Ono, was protected by a plexiglass box. (The museum was concerned that Beatles' fans might try to make off with pieces of the car, and indeed, though they couldn't get at the car, they repeatedly disappeared with its caption.)

Furniture went into what was once the music room, a French rococo room with gold leaf and ivory trim and parquet floors. The Cooper-Hewitt designers mounted all the 20th-century furniture on white-painted plywood platforms and grouped it along the walls in roughly chronological order. Though the room is potentially overpowering with its ornamentation from another century, the 20th-

century items refused to be intimidated — in particular, a brass and copper bathtub with a hippopotamus's shape, designed in the early 1970s by Claude Lalanne.

In what was once Carnegie's dining room was a table full of 20th-century place settings (mounted beneath plexiglass cases to dissuade visitors from walking off with the silverware). These place settings were

especially hard to round up because no museum collects them, and the Cooper-Hewitt finally resorted to asking its staff members to lend the exhibit their own silver knives and forks. In fact, the entire show had no precedent. No one yet collects many 20th-century ornaments, so most items had to be rounded up one by one from a lengthy list of donors.

Into the old mansion's largest

Photos by T. Rose

1. Rolls Royce donated to Cooper-Hewitt by John Lennon and Yoko Ono.
2. Neon sign.
3. 20th-century furniture in what was once Andrew Carnegie's music room. Hippopotamus-shaped brass and copper bathtub was designed in 1970s by Claude Lalanne.
4. Place settings.

room, with its 15′ ceilings, went the exhibit's architecture. Tall blowups (made with 3M's photomural process) of four major U.S. buildings stood mounted on self-supporting panels and cubes. These four—the Chrysler building, the Woolworth building, the Seagram building and the soon-to-be-completed A. T. & T. building—are all in New York City and all reflect different attitudes toward ornament. All are, of course, ornaments themselves, adorning the island of Manhattan. Near the photos were examples of architectural detailing, many mounted in cases designed for the show, cases the museum will keep and reuse in other exhibits.

Perhaps the exhibit's most diverting display consisted of blowups of 20th-century lips distorted with 20th-century makeup. The lips belonged to four women—Vilma Banky, Joan Crawford, Marilyn Monroe and disco-diva Grace Jones—and all were ornamental. So, of course, was John Lennon's yellow Rolls Royce, which was the artifact most difficult to mount. A Smithsonian rigger winched the car up a ramp through the museum's front door, which it cleared by a scant inch.

The Casebook jurors thought the show "sympathetic to the building" and recognized this first display of 20th-century ornament (which the Cooper-Hewitt is now collecting) as "important."

**Client:** Cooper-Hewitt Museum (New York), the Smithsonian Institution's National Museum of Design
**Design firm:** Cooper-Hewitt design staff
**Designers:** Dorothy Twining Globus, Richard Oliver, Robin Parkinson, Christian Rohlfing
**Fabrication:** Cooper-Hewitt Museum staff

5.

6.

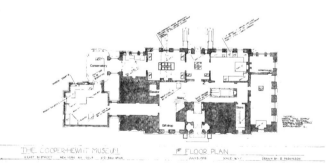

5. 20th-century buildings as ornament.
6. Floor plan.

# The New York School

Like many other architects and designers, Richard Meier is also a painter. He started painting as a young man, and many of his friends and acquaintances are artists. More than that, they are New York artists, artists who, like Meier, live and work in New York City. So, when the New York State Museum in Albany asked architect Meir to design a show of New York School artists —eight weeks before it was scheduled to open—he went to work forthwith with his usual confident enthusiasm. He knew just what he wanted.

Space for the exhibit was a windowless 42,000-sq. ft. hall (a football field has 45,000 square feet) in the Cultural Education Center on the Albany Mall. And though that may seem large, most of the 90-odd works exhibited were huge (the largest canvas was more than 100′ long); and to display them the way he had in mind, Meier needed space. He wanted viewers to be able to see each piece of sculpture, each painting, from

different angles, from different distances, and from different vistas — from "many perspectives," as he put it. He wanted to create an exhibit framework that let viewers glimpse segments of a work on display, then, from a different position, see the whole thing. He wanted the exhibit to be full of excitement and surprise, the way a city is. His exhibit framework is made up of what he sees as streets, alleys, doorways, walks, windows, of circles, cubes, squares and rectangles, suggesting a city. "These people are, in essence, 'street people,'" Meier has said, speaking of the New York School artists, "people of the city with city involvement. They live in an environment of streets, alleys and windows; this design is therefore a city metaphor."

Meir fashioned his exhibit framework out of wood studs and gypsum board, creating walls about 20′ high, beneath the exhibit hall's approximately 35′ ceilings. Essentially, the plan he

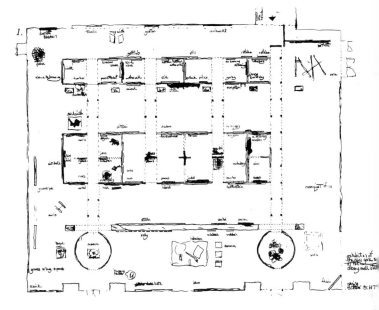

1.

1. *Floor plan sketch includes position of each painting.*
2. *Like a city, exhibit structure had windows, walls and walkways.*

2.

created can be described as a rectangular, roofless 17-room house, flanked by streets and, on one side, a garden wall. Running through the house were three covered walkways, 7½′ high, and running next to the house, past its open-walled, roofless room, was a fourth wall, which led through the garden wall to one of two cylindrical pavilions to display large sculptures: one held Claes Oldenburg's "Soft Fan"; the other, Mark di Suvero's "Martian Ears." "Their form catches the light," Meier says of these cylindrical pavilions, "and acts as a window within the space."

Light came from overhead track lighting out of a black ceiling-sky playing onto the exhibit's white walls.

Though the New York School exhibit ran only a few months, the New York State Museum is maintaining Meier's design of the space, planning to use it for other exhibits.

3.

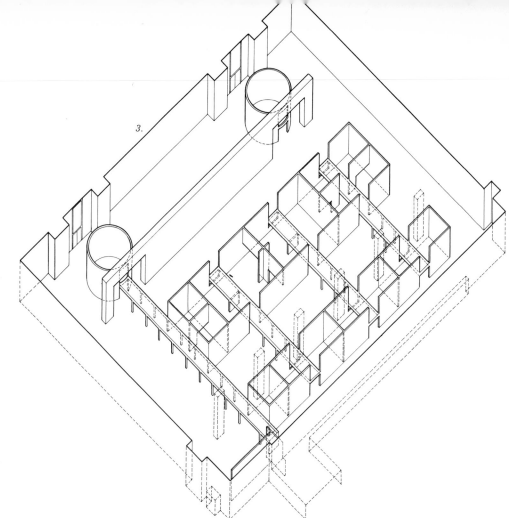

4.

**Client:** State of New York Offices of General Services (Albany); Courtney Sale, director
**Design firm:** Richard Meier and Associates, New York City
**Designers:** Richard Meier; Paul Aferiat and Henry Smith-Miller, assistants
**Curator:** Thomas B. Hess
**Fabricator:** State of New York Office of General Services

*Photos by Ezra Stoller*

5.

3. *Cross-sectional drawing of exhibit plan.*

4-6. *Covered walkways bisect long corridors. Two round pavilions held sculpture.*

6.

# Egyptian Collection
# Phase II

The Metropolitan Museum of Art in New York is two-thirds of the way through a massive redesign of its Egyptian art exhibits. In all, the Metropolitan's Egyptian collection comprises some 45,000 artifacts, collected by the museum since 1874 when the museum's first director, General Luigi Palma de Cesnola, sent five Egyptian objects back from Cyprus in a shipload of artifacts. When the three-phase redesign program is completed, virtually all these 45,000 items will be on display in some 40,000 sq. ft. of space (an acre has 42,560 sq. ft.). None of the collection will be in storage, accessible only to scholars. The recently completed Phase II makes visible to everyone material from a thousand years of Egyptian history, the years 1397 to 380 B.C., from the late-18th dynasty to the 29th dynasty.

Tutankhamun was a late-18th dynasty king; so was Akhenaton, who moved the Egyptian capital from Thebes to Amarna and introduced worship of Ra, the sun god. And the museum has on display, along one entire wall, the materials used in Tutankhamun's embalming. These were found in the desert by Theodore Davis in 1907. Davis, an American businessman and amateur Egyptologist, thought they were items plundered from Tutankhamun's tomb. They were not, of course, and when correctly identified by a member of the Metropolitan Museum's Egyptian Expedition, they helped Howard Carter decide where to dig in his search for the tomb.

All of the Metropolitan's Phase II installation follows the design of Phase I (which was featured in Exhibition Casebook 3). Under

1.

Photos by Stan Ries

2.

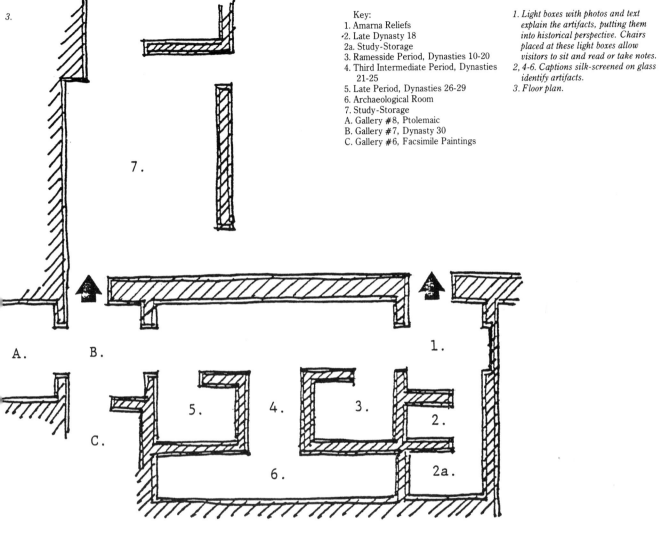

3.

Key:
1. Amarna Reliefs
2. Late Dynasty 18
2a. Study-Storage
3. Ramesside Period, Dynasties 10-20
4. Third Intermediate Period, Dynasties 21-25
5. Late Period, Dynasties 26-29
6. Archaeological Room
7. Study-Storage
A. Gallery #8, Ptolemaic
B. Gallery #7, Dynasty 30
C. Gallery #6, Facsimile Paintings

1. *Light boxes with photos and text explain the artifacts, putting them into historical perspective. Chairs placed at these light boxes allow visitors to sit and read or take notes.*
2, 4-6. *Captions silk-screened on glass identify artifacts.*
3. *Floor plan.*

7.

A.    B.

1.

5.    4.    3.

2.

C.

2a.

6.

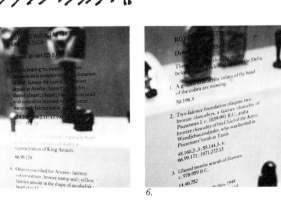

4.

PRIVATE OBJECTS DATING
THE EARLY RAMESSIDE PERIOD

2. Objects Pertaining to the Funerary Cult:

5.

6.

the direction of architects Kevin Roche, John Dinkeloo & Associates, the first floor museum spaces have been given floors of rose-colored granite, approximately the color and texture of Aswan granite. And throughout the exhibit space limestone forms background walls and bases on which sculpture is displayed. Roche purposely kept the materials and colors used in the exhibit design simple and, where possible, in keeping with those found in Egypt. Against the limestone color he added green (in a carpet, which runs through the exhibit space) to evoke the green strip of vegetation running along the Nile. Though some of the larger artifacts stand alone in handsomely detailed cases of tempered glass with their own light source, most of the artifacts are positioned in 8'-high cases of tempered glass and steel (also with their own lighting), which undulate along the walls, projecting slightly into the room here, retreating there, creating supple and continuous glassed-in exhibit space.

Designer Roche wanted large continuous cases so he wouldn't have to mount everything separately on pedestals, and these cases are wide enough for curators to walk into and position artifacts. Within each case, in back of a vertical partition, is a 30″ width left for carts carrying heavier artifacts. All cases have controlled temperature, humidity and dust levels.

In each of the six galleries of the Phase II installation is a light box (20″ wide, put together in 4′ sections) of the same elegant steel and glass found in the cases. In these boxes, using transparencies of maps, artifacts and diagrams coupled with blocks

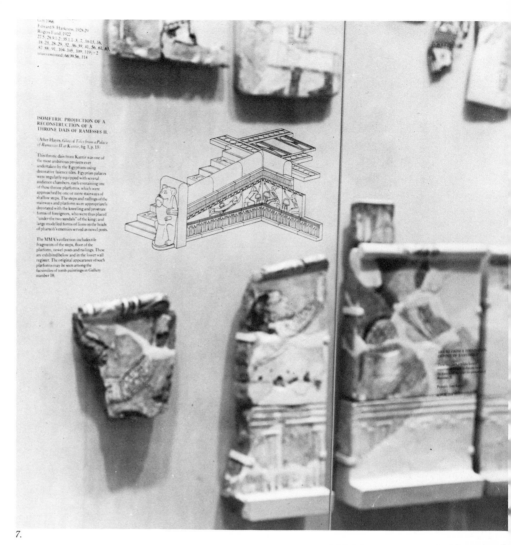

7.

8.

Photo by Arthur Rosenblatt

9.

10.

of white-on-black Caslon type, graphic designer Rudolph de Harak gives visitors a chance to study what they see around them. Though some of the Casebook jurors objected to the descriptive material being placed across the room from the artifacts described (the light boxes are either hung on a wall or set up as tables with bentwood chairs positioned along their length), they praised the exhibit's elegance and the fact that the museum is taking all its Egyptian artifacts out of storage and putting them on display. "Children come into the museum on weekends and you can find them with their notebooks on the lightboxes taking notes," says Arthur Rosenblatt, the museum's vice president in charge of architecture and planning.

The second phase of the installation cost $2,000,000. The third phase is expected to be open by late 1980 or early 1981.

7. *Looking into one of the 8'-high wall cases.*
8. *Some of the light boxes are hung on the walls, to be read standing up.*
9. *Wall cases beyond light box.*
10. *Visitors pass through Egyptian Collection to reach Temple of Dendur, permanently installed in new wing of museum.*

**Client:** Metropolitan Museum of Art (New York); Arthur Rosenblatt, vice president, architecture and planning
**Design firm:** Kevin Roche, John Dinkeloo & Associates, Hamden, CT; Rudolph de Harak Associates (graphics)
**Designers:** Kevin Roche, Rudolph de Harak, New York City (graphics)
**Installation:** Thomas Logan, associate curator, Department of Egyptian Art; Peter Dorman, Cathleen Keeler, Yitzhak Margowsky, Edna R. Russmann, and members of the conservation departments.

# British Genius Exhibition

In the past 100 years the British have given the world rayon (1883), the steam turbine (1884), the radio tube diode (1905), stainless steel (1916), the tank (1914) and penicillin (1929). These and other British technical inventions and scientific discoveries of the past 100 years were celebrated in the "British Genius Exhibition" which stood under a tent in London's Battersea Park during the summer and fall of 1978. Sponsored by the John Player Foundation, which put up approximately 1½ million dollars for it, the exhibit actually appeared beneath two tents. One, which the designers called an experimental structure, covered a refreshment kiosk and a coat check room. The main tent was circular, like a circus tent, suspended from a central mast, covering 10,000 sq. ft. of exhibit area on two levels.

Visitors entered this main tent past four period displays, moving into a central area devoted mostly to displays of British scientific discoveries during the 25-year reign of Queen Elizabeth II. Exhibit devices included a 12-screen motion picture, static exhibits with mannikins, and a welter of disc-shaped photo and text panels. Though one Casebook juror found the results chaotic, the rest thought the material was presented with a sense of humor and that the disparity of forms, shapes and materials, which elsewhere might have led to disorder, worked well here. The graphics, they felt, were especially good.

The designers invented a stencil typeface, which they used throughout, on signs. Texts were done in typewriter fonts.

Most of the work on the exhibit was done in the two months before it opened, and that it did open on schedule was because of a flurry of late work, often in the rain.

*1.*

THE OBSSESSIVE INVENTOR

'...THE FANATICAL ENTHUSIASM IS THE OUTCOME OF A CREATIVE DRIVE, THE SUCCESS IS THE RESULT OF CERTAIN ESSENTIAL ELEMENTS OF CHARACTER'
H S HATFIELD

*2.*

1. Disc-shaped panel inside tent.
2. Exhibit appeared beneath two tents in London's Battersea Park: one held refreshment stands and coat-check space; the other held the main displays on two levels.
3. Designers invented a stencil typeface for signs and banners.

EXIT
TOILETS
REFRESHMENTS

IN THE INTERESTS OF
PUBLIC SAFETY ALL HAND
LUGGAGE MUST BE
SUBMITTED FOR
INSPECTION.
BRIEFCASES, PARCELS,
UMBRELLAS, WALKING
STICKS MUST BE
DEPOSITED IN THE
CLOAKROOM
THE MANAGEMENT
RESERVES THE RIGHT TO
REFUSE ADMISSION

3.

MORECAMBE
& WISE
BY NICHOLAS MUNRO

4.

**Client:** Carlton Cleere Ltd., on behalf of the John Player Foundation
**Design firm:** Pentagram Design, London
**Consultants:** Buro Happold, tent design; Viscom, 12-screen audiovisual; Nicholas Munro, sculpture
**Fabricator:** Russell Bros.

4. *Period rooms help tell the story of British inventions.*
5, 6. *So do motion pictures and buttons.*

5.

EXHIBITION CONTINUES  NEXT AUDIO VISUAL SHOW IN          MINUTES

'THE LIVING RACE IS
THE INHERITOR OF THE INDUSTRY
AND SKILL OF ALL PAST TIMES AND
THE CIVILISATION WE ENJOY
IS BUT THE SUM OF THE
USEFUL EFFECTS OF LABOUR
DURING THE PAST CENTURIES'
SAMUEL SMILES 1863

# British Columbia
# Provincial Museum Train

The idea of a train to pull exhibits through the countryside, making them available to people in small towns who would probably never know they exist, much less go somewhere to see one, is not a new idea. Manitoba has a museum train, for instance, and in 1976 the U.S. had its Bicentennial American Freedom Train. But the idea is sound and exciting and not yet overworked.

During the summers of 1978 and 1979 the British Columbia Provincial Museum Train moved out of Victoria and into the provincial towns, pulling exhibits mounted in old railway passenger cars. Most recently, in 1979, there were three exhibit cars for two exhibits, one on Captain James Cook, who on his last voyage 200 years ago explored and charted the coast of what is now British Columbia, and one exhibit on steam power and its role in the development of British Columbia from the 1830s to the 1960s. A fourth coach held a theater where two 12-minute movies, one on Cook, one on steam, played continuously.

In any train exhibit, space is, of course, limited, not only for the exhibits but also for the people viewing them. Crowding becomes a paramount problem. The British Columbia Provincial Museum designers handled crowding by giving people waiting to board the museum train something to look at outside: an exhibit mounted on flat cars — an 8'-high steam locomotive, used in lumbering, rides on one car and a boiler on another. But the hit of this outside show may have been the museum train's own locomotive, a 2-8-2 steam locomotive, No. 3716, greased and painted and restored by Bob Swanson. People had plenty to look at

1.

2.

1. Floor plans of the museum train's four exhibit cars.
2. Designer Tom Putnam with model of the James Cook exhibit.
3. Museum train poster.
4, 5. The museum train's steam locomotive is the traveling exhibit's star attraction.

outside and plenty of room to see it in until their turn came to move inside.

Inside, there was plenty, too. Designer Thomas L. Putnam used dioramas, models, artifacts and photomurals to tell his two stories. In the "Steampower and British Columbia" cars, each about 80′ long and 9′ wide with 6′ platforms at either end, Putnam had permanent walls installed covering all windows except one; the latter was left uncovered to avoid the claustrophobic feeling the enclosed 630-sq. ft. space might induce. Next to the uncovered window (each exhibit car had one) he put a club car chair, covered in suede vinyl. Suede vinyl covered the walls, too, colored variously gray, blue, rust or natural, depending on the historical era of the display in front of it.

3.

4.

5.

Putnam also designed the carpet and had it woven in wool, using the wall colors and adding black-and-white. Stripes in the carpet were meant to convey the feeling of railway tracks and emphasize the cars' long, narrow shape. Though he wanted to display some of the larger steam engines and equipment used in British Columbia during its age of steam — for example, the "Iron Chink," a steam-powered fish-cutting machine used in fisheries in place of the Chinese laborers who usually did the work — Putnam found it impossible to get them through the cars' 28"-wide doors and had to settle for scale models. Models and dioramas were in plexiglass cases lighted by Halo "lovo" lighting and electrified railway lanterns. Overhead lighting came from light tracks.

Because the walls were permanent, train crews had trouble replacing windows broken by small boys with stones and large men with small minds and guns as the train moved through cities and countryside. So, in the James Cook exhibit car, added in honor of the bicentennial of Cook's voyage along the British Columbia coast, walls were removable, constructed of an artist's-type canvas glued to wooden frames, which were attached top and bottom to two-by-fours to form modular panels. Canvas was sprayed with a natural canvas-color latex paint so it could be kept clean.

Showcases holding models, dioramas and artifacts, such as a facsimile of the dagger used to kill Cook, looked nautical. They had teakwood floors, canvas-covered wooden frames, plexiglass fronts and sturdy,

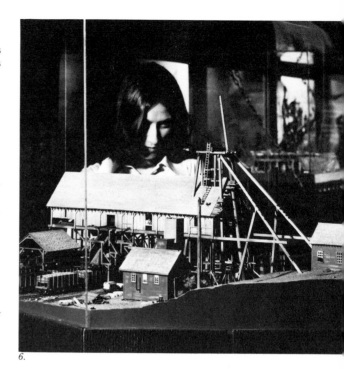

6.

7.

teak, waist-level railings. In one was a model of Cook's ship; in another, a model of a 1778 Indian village at Nootka Sound, B.C., designed from original drawings. There were navigational instruments, sailmaking tools, a map of Cook's three voyages, and more—though the designers carefully calculated the amount of material displayed so that visitors could take it in without holding up those waiting to enter.

Putnam chose a Goudy Old Style typeface for the Cook exhibit because it speaks of tradition and a Palatino in the steam exhibit because it tied in with typefaces used in the museum.

For 13 years before the museum train came along, Putnam had designed permanent exhibits for the museum, working with the usual army of designers, technicians and curators needed for such vast projects. He found the museum train exciting not just because of the subject but also because of the chance to control, on his own, both the exhibit design and its installation. The Casebook jurors shared his excitement, calling the train and its exhibits an "impressive piece of work."

**Client:** British Columbia Provincial Museum (Victoria, B.C.)
**Design firm:** Exhibits Division, British Columbia Provincial Museum
**Designers:** Tom Putnam; Royle Harris, John Robertson (graphics)
**Consultants:** Railway Appliance Research Ltd., Bob Swanson (rolling stock and locomotive restoration); Lindsay Models and Design Consultants (steam diorama models); Epp and Vissar Ltd. (steamship models); George Hearne (scale-model locomotives); Osbourne Orr Ltd. (steam exhibit carpet); Four Seasons Fabric Ltd. (steam exhibit wall coverings); Carl Chaplin (steam exhibit poster artist)
**Fabricator:** Western Display Service Ltd.

8.

9.

10.

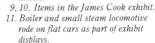

6-8. British Columbia and steampower exhibit.
9, 10. Items in the James Cook exhibit.
11. Boiler and small steam locomotive rode on flat cars as part of exhibit displays.

11.

# Two Costume Exhibits:
# Vanity Fair/Ballet Russes

Over a period of two years, two major costume shows flared forth in the usually more staid galleries of New York's Metropolitan Museum of Art. Gleaned from the museum's 30,000-item clothing and accessories collection by Diana Vreeland, former editor of Vogue, the shows were highly theatrical, flashy, sometimes dazzling, not reflecting what Lucian J. Leone, the Metropolitan's exhibit designer, who designed the installations, calls wryly "the usual beige museum mentality." Rather, they reflected Mrs. Vreeland's committment to "excitement," a term she used to indicate creation of an atmosphere dazzling enough to disguise a lack of conventional organization. But any seeming lack of organization was carefully calculated to leave visitors feeling they hadn't seen it all and wanting to hurry back.

## Vanity Fair: A Treasure Trove from the Costume Institute

"Vanity Fair" displayed some 500 items of clothing from the Metropolitan Museum of Art's Costume Institute collection. They were given 6000 sq. ft. of space beneath a 10' ceiling in the museum's multi-chambered costume galleries. In places, designer Leone and special consultant Vreeland tried to give the impression of a higher ceiling by putting vertically striped upholstery fabric on the walls. But mostly, the exhibit flowed horizontally through the space. Each gallery had its own wall fabric scheme or special color, producing with the costumes in place a cornucopia of texture and color. Fabrics not only draped mannikins but also were tacked

tightly across frameworks of battens erected against the walls. "If we'd had the money," says Leone, whose design budget was $75,000, "we probably would have upholstered everything."

All mannikins stood on platforms, raised slightly off the floor, and these 4' by 4' modular platforms were covered with fabric (mostly exhibit felt in 6" widths). Where the walls weren't fabriced, they were painted in bold, arresting colors: lavender, acid green, deep wine, yellow. Mannikins, too, were either brightly painted or covered with dyed stretch fabrics.

In a gallery whose walls were lined with a flowered fabric were more than 50 examples of 19th-century American and European lingerie — gowns and peignoirs made from muslin, cambric, lawn and dimity garnished with ruffles, ribbons and laces. Elsewhere there were court dresses, feather dresses, ball gowns, parasols, jewelry, shoes, men's embroidered vests, opulent Chinese robes, ribbons, combs and lace. Golden hands held hangers in racks full of clothes. Spotlights washed shimmering silver-colored mannikins wearing silver-colored gowns. There were satin and brocade dresses that once belonged to Turkish girls and suits once worn by the Duke of Windsor. To help set the mood for all this color and fabric, New York musicologist Stuart Pivar compiled a tape which, according to the museum, expressed the exhibit's "many aspects, moods and geographical flavors."

A grant from the International Telephone & Telegraph Corporation made the exhibit possible.

*Vanity Fair costumes.*

## Diaghilev: Costumes and Designs for the Ballet Russes

Because of its subject this costume show had more apparent organization than its predecessor, "Vanity Fair," at the Metropolitan Museum of Art in New York. The Russian impresario Sergei Pavlovich Diaghilev profoundly altered the art and fashion of his time when, in 1909, his troupe performed at the Theatre du Chatelet in Paris. The music of the Russian composers had bold rhythms, and the colors of Diaghilev's sets and costumes were bold, too — reds, oranges, purples. Special consultant Diana Vreeland wanted to recreate the sensation of that first performance, and the 100 costumes accompanied by sketches, postures, costume and stage designs from major Ballet Russes productions — many on loan from London's Victoria and Albert Museum, the Los Angeles County Museum of Art and the private collection of Robert Tobin in San Antonio — were arranged loosely according to specific productions. There was a "Sleeping Princess" setting, for instance, a "Scheherazade," and a "Firebird" gallery, in which a particular ballet was central to the mood and color.

Ambience couldn't be created so much by color and texture as in the "Vanity Fair" show, much of whose fabric was donated, and to meet the $90,000 design budget Metropolitan exhibit designer Lucian J. Leone and Vreeland relied more on lighting and music. They simplified the fabric treatment and color schemes, they say, but what remained could hardly be described as timid or retiring. Colors were lavender, deep blue, wine red, Chinese red. To save money they repeated colors (three galleries were lavender, for instance), instead of trying to give each gallery a different color or fabric treatment.

There were mannikin-mounted costumes worn by Nijinsky in "Swan Lake," "Le Dieu Bleu" and "Petrouchka," and costumes designed by Matisse for the 1920 production of Stravinsky's "Le Chant du Rossignol." Tapes played music from the great ballets, music composed by Stravinsky, Tchaikovsky, Rimsky-Korsakov, Debussy; and throughout, the light intensity changed continuously. Lighting designer Lemar Terry used colored gells revolving in front of spots to change color and intensity. On a red wall in the "Firebird" ballet gallery a northern-lights effect played over the wall. On mannikins in the "Sleeping Beauty" gallery light changed sequentially, lighting one mannikin brightly, a second warmly and a third darkly in alternating sequence. In the "Scheherazade" gallery the light was almost garish, flashing and rebounding off gold lamé.

**Client:** Metropolitan Museum of Art (New York)
**Design firm:** Design Department, Metropolitan Museum of Art; Herbert F. Schmidt, head of exhibition design
**Designer:** Lucian J. Leone
**Organizer:** Diana Vreeland, special consultant to the Costume Institute, Metropolitan Museum of Art
**Consultants:** Lemar Terry, lighting designer, Metropolitan Museum of Art; Stuart Pivar, musicologist (Vanity Fair); Stephen Paley, music (Ballet Russes); Victoria and Albert Museum (Ballet Russes); staff and volunteers of the Costume Institute, Metropolitan Museum of Art
**Fabricators:** Building Department, Metropolitan Museum of Art; General Drapery Services, Inc.

*Ballet Russes costumes.*

# Splendors of Dresden

Many experts maintain that the collecting of art treasures, as we know it, started in Dresden in about 1500, and the exhibit "Splendors of Dresden," which toured the U.S. in 1978 and '79, appearing in three museums during that time, was designed not only to show off Dresden's art treasures but also the way these treasures had been collected and displayed throughout five centuries. Ten institutions in Dresden under the banner of the State Art Collection of Dresden cooperated, in putting the show together, with the three U.S. institutions: the National Gallery of Art, the Metropolitan Museum of Art and the Fine Arts Museum of San Francisco. The idea for the show originated almost simultaneously in the U.S. and the German Democratic Republic when the two countries first established diplomatic relations in 1974. With the opening of the new East German embassy in Washington, in the summer of 1975, the East German ambassador brought up the idea of such an exhibit with the National Gallery's director, only to find that the director had requested State Department permission to work toward such an exhibit the summer before.

But if the conception was easy, the fruition was not, for the designers and curators had to portray as frozen in time exhibit settings which had been changing continuously through the centuries, and then were mostly destroyed by bombing in World War II. Working predominantly with 19th-century drawings, designers from the National Gallery of Art prepared models (to 1″ and ½″ scale) of the proposed settings. These settings, recreating portions of

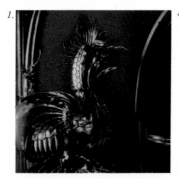

The Porcelain Collection

1-3. Dresden bronzes.
4. The Porcelain collection.
5. The Green Vault.
6. Jousting knights herald the Dresden exhibit at the bottom of the National Gallery's stair lobby.
7. Floor plan. Exhibit was arranged in 24 rooms.

7.

Dresden's museums and display rooms, were suggested by Dresden curators under the leadership of Joachim Menzhausen, director of Dresden's Green Vault, who National Gallery designer Gaillard Ravenel calls simply "one of the most brilliant persons we have worked with." When the National Gallery designers had their scale models ready, they carried photographs of them to Dresden for a curatorial critique. "This must be a half inch further this way," the curators would say, or "This should be standing next to that." Not all items in the show were arranged sequentially, though attention was paid to general sequence. What predominated was the settings. One, for instance, a setting for 200 pieces of porcelain, was based on 18th-century drawings of the Japanese Palace, the four-winged building on the banks of the Elbe, which was to have been Augustus the Strong's porcelain palace. (He died even before its exterior was completed.) Another, the Kunstkammer, or "cabinet of curiosities," the name given to the private museums some German princes began to establish after 1500, is taken from 16th-century drawings. Yet another setting, The Rustkammer, containing weapons and military equipment, jeweled swords, inlaid pistols, powder flasks, and crossbows, is based on 19th-century photographs of Dresden's Armor Museum. And still another, the Green Vault with its mirrored wall niche and mirrored cabinets holding objects of gold and silver often encrusted with jewels, is a recreation of a section of a larger room (one of eight in the existing Green Vault) designed with

detailed information taken from architectural drawings used to restore Dresden's Green Vaults after the 1945 bombing.

Design of the exhibit was further complicated because none of the spaces in the three museums it was to travel to would be the same. In partial solution to this problem, the National Gallery designers designed three entire rooms (Kunstkammer, Green Vault, porcelain room) to be taken apart and shipped, with their air-conditioning ducts, their wiring, their lighting and their display devices. Their walls, beams, trusses, joists and ducts were bolted together; architectural moldings hid seams. Temperature-and-humidity-controlled air circulated through the rooms, entering through floor-level vents, hidden behind cases and shelves, and leaving through slots hidden by crown moldings at the tops of walls. All small objects in the exhibit were shielded by plexiglass, sometimes hung from attachments within nonstructural overhead beams to rest in floor grooves. All artifact lighting was positioned behind these sheets.

Obviously, none of the settings could be more than amalgams of the settings found over a period of centuries in Dresden. As noted, for instance, the exhibit's single porcelain room was a distillation of the entire Japanese Palace. And the Kunstkammer, as it originally existed in 16th-century Dresden, had been seven massive rooms; as it toured the U.S., it was a single room cut in half, with one window instead of two, to give more display space. Its design was not taken from any one Kunstkammer as it existed in any one year, but rather from

8.

8, 9. Kunstkammer.
10. Dresden statues.
11. Entrance to the Armory or Rustkammer.

9.

several. It was designed piecemeal from old drawings, from the design of existing Kunstkammers in other Saxon cities, and from descriptions in travel diaries. The room's wall decoration was taken from Martin Luther's library in Wittenburg, not far from Dresden.

So it was with the other settings. The ambience they created was as important to the designers as was the presence of any one artifact. "The point of the installation," says a National Gallery spokesman, "was to impress a visitor with the incredible splendor of a Renaissance curiosity cabinet." For this reason, the designers avoided labels entirely. Instead, each visitor could take with him a free brochure describing the exhibit's items as he moved through the rooms. In all, there were some 800 objects arranged in 18,000 sq. ft. at the National Gallery, divided there into 24 rooms. And all these rooms were replicas of Dresden museum space. Some made concessions to contemporary exhibit display. For instance, instead of hanging the exhibit's fine Old-Master paintings as they had been hung in the 18th century in Dresden's Stallhof, a gallery converted from the royal stables, ceiling to floor and corner to corner, they were displayed at eye level, generously spaced in five galleries.

The entire National Gallery installation was tucked into the Gallery's temporary exhibition space, whose entrance is beneath a cantilevered section of the East Building's main floor, at the bottom of a five-story stair lobby. Into this open space the designers brought out part of the show. There, on the floor, two armored knights on prancing pâpier-maché horses faced one another, lances and plumes in place. Lured down to inspect these warriors, visitors could see two immense photomurals tucked beneath the first floor overhang, one of ancient Dresden, one of the knights on horseback, urging visitors on toward the exhibit entrance. Beyond the entrance, the show began with a painting prophesying the destruction to be brought about by Fascism.

Money for the "Splendors of Dresden" came mainly from IBM. But others contributed, too: the Robert Wood Johnson, Jr., Charitable Trust, the National Endowment for the Arts, the National Endowment for the Humanities, and the Museum Society of the Fine Arts Museums of San Francisco.

10.

11.

**Clients:** National Gallery of Art; Metropolitan Museum of Art; Fine Arts Museum of San Francisco.
**Design firm:** Design Department, National Gallery of Art
**Designers:** Gaillard F. Ravenel, Mark Leithauser, Elroy Quenroe
**Writer:** William J. William, National Gallery of Art.
**Fabricators:** Design and Production; Russell-William

# Aquatic Exotic

It was one of those rare projects that went without a hitch. Up to a point. The point came about a week before the "Aquatic Exotic" exhibit's public opening in the British Columbia Provincial Museum. Staff designer Roy Harris looked up from installing his special light boxes in the museum's 6000-sq. ft. temporary gallery to see workmen trucking wheelbarrows of cement past him, cement for major renovation work throughout the building. That trucking went on for several days, but Harris's luck turned two days before the opening when the renovation quieted, and he was able to clean up.

From the Provincial Museum, "Aquatic Exotic" will travel for three years to National Museum Exhibit centers across Canada. Moving by museum truck, the exhibit, 28′ long and 12′ wide, is designed to be taken down by one man, slipped into black vinyl traveling cases and put aboard the truck in packages weighing from 25 to 50 pounds each.

Set up, the exhibit consists of 15 light boxes arranged in museum space of 800 sq. ft. or more. These light boxes, made of translucent opal acrylic to glow from the light of internal fluorescent fixtures, are shaped with peaks and steps, like gardens of undersea coral, holding color transparencies of British Columbia marine life. In all, there are 40 underwater photographs, of sea slugs and sea stars, of anemone, coral, jellyfish, eels and fish such as greenlings, cod and sole. Some of these Cibachrome transparencies are blown up to 30″ by 60″, some to 24″ by 30″, and some are 8″ by 10″; all are placed between two sheets of

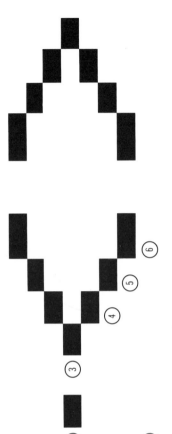

*1.*

Key:
1. Exhibit Hall
2. Title and copy panel
3. Photo 30″ × 60″
4. Group copy panel
5. 20″ × 30″ photo panel
6. Eight photos 8″ × 10″

*1. Plan.*
*2-9. Set up in a darkened or semi-darkened room, faceted, opal-colored light boxes glow dramatically. Enlarged transparencies set onto the boxes' sloping tops provide color.*

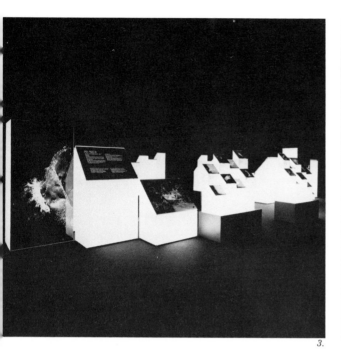

3.

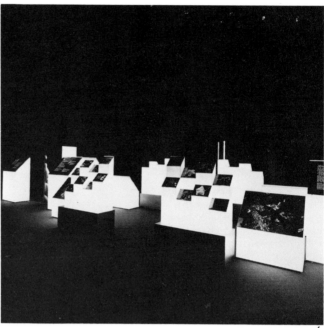

4.

6.

7.

clear ½" acrylic and attached to the light boxes. Harris designed special fastenings for the light boxes that allow a workman, or "handler," the exhibit's travelling guardian, to put the light box sections together without tools. Fluorescent lighting fixtures are fastened to a plywood piece forming the bottom of each light box. And the boxes' wiring interconnects so that they can be connected to one another in varying patterns depending on the requirements of a particular museum space, then plugged into a single outlet with a single cord.

Though some of the peaks and crests of these light boxes may rise as high as 5′, viewing surfaces are generally 30″ or 32″ off the floor, glowing attractively at the audiences, largely children, who come to view it.

Captions are silk-screened onto the acrylic surfaces. Harris chose a University Light typeface for headings and Tiffany for text copy, because they're legible and slightly exotic, like the marine animals in the photos. Next to some of the photos are life-sized drawings of the animals, for scale, because the photos of tiny organisms tend to make them seem huge.

The museum staff considered two alternative exhibit formats. Initially they thought of displaying three-dimensional models of at least some of the marine animals, but discarded the idea because they had only three months before the exhibit opening. The second alternative was to use a panel system, creating a series of unlighted rooms in which photos would be displayed on the walls. But Harris had been toying with the idea of glowing light boxes and seized the chance to try it out.

His boxes work equally well, he maintains, in a dark room and in one with ambient light.

He put the exhibit together for $10,000, slightly less than the maximum budget the museum allowed.

"Elegant" and "sophisticated" the Casebook jurors called it. "It's compact," they noted, "and has lots of style."

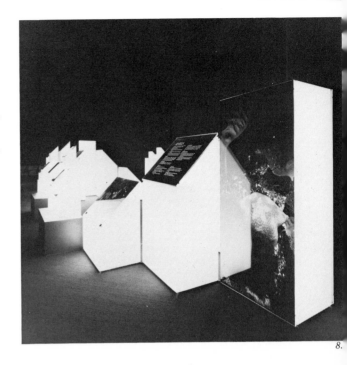

8.

**Client:** British Columbia Provincial Museum (Victoria, B.C.)
**Design firm:** Exhibits Division, British Columbia Provincial Museum
**Designers:** Roy Harris; Brent Cooke, photography
**Fabricator:** Robert Byers

9.

# Pompeii AD 79

1. Exhibit logo.
2. Roman statue.
3. Plaster replica of female charred by
   Vesuvius's lava.

The 350 examples of Roman paintings, mosaics, sculpture, coins, furniture, pottery, jewelry and tools on display for four months in New York's American Museum of Natural History were probably more suited to display and interpretation by a natural history museum than by an art museum. Before arriving in New York, the traveling exhibit, on loan from the National Archeological Museum in Naples, Italy, and the Antiquarium in Pompeii, had visited art museums in Europe and the U.S. (Boston, Chicago, Dallas) where the artifacts were mostly displayed and viewed as art. But though many of the items were unquestionably beautiful, as a whole they more closely represented archeology than art, and the American Museum gave them a broader context.

Captions in Optima type, chosen because it matched the show's logo ("Pompeii AD 79" in hand-drawn letters), explained each artifact's craftsmanship, use and significance in the daily life of Pompeii 1900 years ago. Much of this information had been available in catalogues at other museums, and indeed in setting up its installation, the American Museum leaned heavily on the exhibit catalogue prepared by Boston's Museum of Fine Arts. But the American Museum didn't want to count on visitors buying a catalogue to understand the exhibit. Several large panels of text on the wall established relationships between individual artifacts and, further, between the objects and everyday life in Pompeii.

The American Museum designers, working with about 7000 sq. ft. of open, uninterrupted space, used color

1.

2.

3.

to help visitors follow the exhibit's organization. These colors (echoing colors found in Pompeii, such as the burnished red of tile roofs) painted on the walls delineated seven basic subject areas (for food, jewelry, housing, etc.) and divisions throughout the space were further defined by plants.

George S. Gardner, the museum's chairman of exhibits and design, credits the Victorian precedent of the potted palm for the idea, but he says, too, that more recently he was reminded of the usefulness of plant dividers by a Bicentennial exhibit at the Smithsonian. In the American Museum's Pompeii exhibit plants are Mediterranean, plants that might have appeared in Pompeii: small palms, ficus 8′ to 10′ high, and ivy, spotted throughout the gallery for visual relief and orientation. Circulation at the American Museum was aided by the gallery's configuration, a large open room with an entrance at one end and an exit at the other. The exhibit's two largest displays, a Pompeiian house recreated at 1/20th scale, and a peristyle, with its columns, pool (in which visitors of course threw coins) a::d a fringe of tile roof, stood toward the center of the room. Visitors flowed around these, past artifacts hung on the surrounding walls and other floor exhibits in plexiglass cases. All the gallery's light came from ceiling-mounted framing spots that picked out and highlighted artifacts and captions. The intense wash of light on the peristyle came from light bounced off a blue ceiling cloth.

Because of its emphasis on the way Pompeiians lived, the American Museum reserved until the end its reminder of how they died, of why Pompeii's life

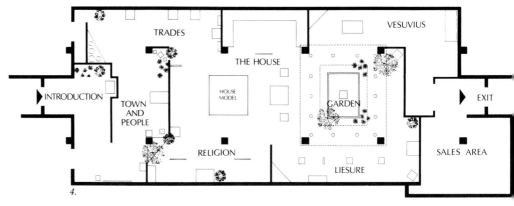

4.

4. Floor plan.
5, 7. Exhibit was lighted entirely by ceiling-mounted framing spots that picked out individual artifacts. American Museum set up exhibit to explain through artifacts how people lived in Pompeii in A.D. 79.
6. Catalogue cover.

5.

# POMPEII AD 79

6.

has been frozen in time and so carefully preserved for 1900 years. Just before visitors passed out of the exhibit into the sales area beyond, they watched a film taken by the U.S. Army during World War II (and borrowed from Dallas's Fine Arts Museum) of the 1944 Vesuvius eruption. The black-and-white film trembled and flickered on its small screen, as if shaken by the eruption, and just beyond it were plastic replicas of a dog and a woman charred by Vesuvius's lava in A.D. 79.

During its first 14 weeks in New York, "Pompeii AD 79," which was arranged by the Italian Ministry of Culture and partially supported by grants from the National Endowment for the Humanities and the Xerox

Corporation, drew more than half a million persons, and though the gallery was crowded on weekends the crowding was not untoward during the rest of the week. Accommodating large, dramatic exhibits such as this has become an American Museum policy in the past few years. In 1976, New York City cut back its support of the museum, withholding money the museum was using to create major, permanent halls. Now, instead, the museum hopes to have one or two large, popular exhibits a year, what the museum calls "special" exhibits that can attract enough paying traffic to aid the museum financially.

Pompeii may not have been an immediate money-maker, for the museum put up $1.1 million of its

own money to present it. But the exhibit helped boost membership. (Members were given ticket priority during the exhibit's four-month run.) In 1976, the museum built a 10,000 sq. ft. gallery for these special exhibits and has seen its exhibition attendance increase 40 per cent since then. During the run of "Pompeii AD 79" alone, the museum doubled its number of participating members.

**Client:** American Museum of Natural History (New York)
**Staff design:** George S. Gardner, art director
**Designer:** Joseph M. Sedacca
**Consultant:** Howard Branston, lighting
**Fabricators:** American Museum of Natural History staff; Lynch, CDI; DeLuca LaCapra Exhibits, Inc.

## Great Treasures of the City

New York is, among other things, a city of museums, and a hint of the riches held by five of them was seen by patrons of the Bowery Savings Bank during 1979. A Frank Lloyd Wright-designed chair, quilted wall hangings, 19th-century toys, gems, fossils, and photos of illuminated manuscripts appeared in exhibits in Bowery Bank lobbies, where these artifacts were exposed to persons who might never think of entering a museum. The Bowery, which has made a policy of promoting New York City, eagerly courted the chance to get some museum artifacts out of the museums and into the bank.

But since museums are, quite understandably, protective of their treasures, the Bowery soon realized it needed a design professional to handle the project reassuringly: to coordinate the exhibit's design, to see that the museums released the necessary artifacts on schedule and to move the exhibits to and set them up in the five Bowery branches. This design professional, William Kissiloff of Kissiloff Associates, worked as a sort of ambassador with portfolio, as designer and intermediary between the bank and the museums.

The five city museums donating material for the exhibit were: the Museum of the City of New York, the American Museum of Natural History, the Cooper-Hewitt Museum, the Museum of Contemporary Crafts, and the New York Public Library. Kissiloff designed free-standing plexiglass cases to house some of the artifacts and mounted others in smaller plexiglass cases fastened over panels suspended from a standard metal exhibit

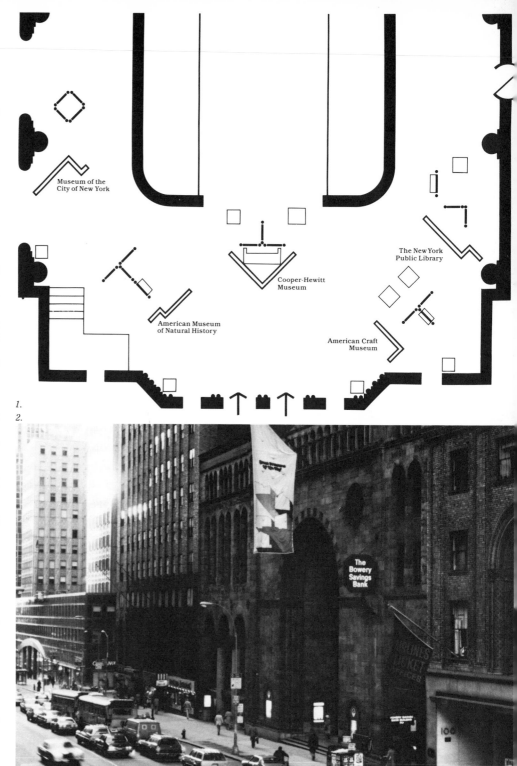

1.

2.

1. *Floor plan of initial exhibit in the Grand Hall of the Bowery Savings Bank 42nd Street branch in Manhattan.*
2. *Banner outside bank proclaims exhibit within.*
3. *Twelve-foot-high blowup of each institution's facade introduces its exhibit. This one is of the American Museum.*

3.

framework, 7' high and 3' wide (System 8). These frameworks also held spotlights and the panels often displayed graphics: photos, text and captions—set in Bookman type, chosen because of its look of quality, its legibility, and because Kissiloff wanted a serif typeface.

Kissiloff designed his cases and panels to be adaptable so they could stand separately or together, giving them enough flexibility to fit in any sequence in any Bowery lobby. Kissiloff's problems were compounded because the exhibit was really six separate exhibits. It appeared first in the Great Hall, the huge banking space of the Bowery Savings Bank on Manhattan's 42nd Street. Here, the displays of all five participating institutions were gathered in one exhibit covering 2,500 sq. ft. Then the act broke up, and each museum's exhibit traveled separately, expanded slightly to cover 900 sq. ft. on its own in Bowery branches throughout the city.

To make the exhibit cohesive, Kissiloff hit on the idea of having a 12'-high blowup of each institution's facade mounted on masonite, standing as an introduction before each exhibit. And he designed special light standards to illuminate these facades from the corners of the exhibit space.

Before setting up each exhibit Kissiloff prowled the banking floor, asking which cashier's windows were open when and where the hidden security cameras were. Then, he arranged the components of his exhibits so that they didn't interfere with normal banking operations. Kissiloff Associates also designed promotional material for the exhibits:

banners, posters and handouts.

In most cases, Kissiloff worked with the directors of the museums involved. But at the American Museum of Natural History he worked directly with George Gardner, chairman of the museum's department of exhibitions and graphics. Gardner had been approached by the Bowery when the bank first conceived the exhibit, and by the time Kissiloff had been appointed to coordinate and design the show, Gardner and his designer, Ralph Applebaum, had almost completed their section of the exhibit. The Gardner-Applebaum solution relies solely on the standard exhibit framework (System 8). Plexiglass cases, mounted directly over graphic panels, hold skeletons, mounted birds, fossils, and other treasures from the museum's collections. Some of these items are so fragile that whenever the exhibit moved from one Bowery branch to another a museum preparator went with it to see that the cases rode comfortably between destinations and were put up properly once they arrived.

The exhibits did several things besides prove the Bowery's public spirit. It took treasures out of museums and gave them a wider audience, and it served as a lure for the museums, perhaps teasing people who, surrounded by culture, never thought about it, into visiting its local storehouses.

**Client:** Bowery Savings Bank (New York City)
**Design firm:** Kissiloff Associates, New York City
**Designers:** William Kissiloff, Wilson Wright, Beatrice Taggart, Edmund Puches, George S. Gardner (art director), Ralph Applebaum
**Fabricator:** CD Industries

*4, 5. A mounted Blue Bird of Paradise and Frank Lloyd Wright-designed chair were two of the Treasures of the City that appeared in bank lobbies.*
*6. System 8 frame with attached lights held graphics and artifacts mounted in plastic cases.*
*7, 8. Exhibit announcement.*
*9. Blowup of facade of Museum of City of New York.*
*10. Visitor views Cooper-Hewitt porcelain exhibit.*

5.

4.

6.

7.

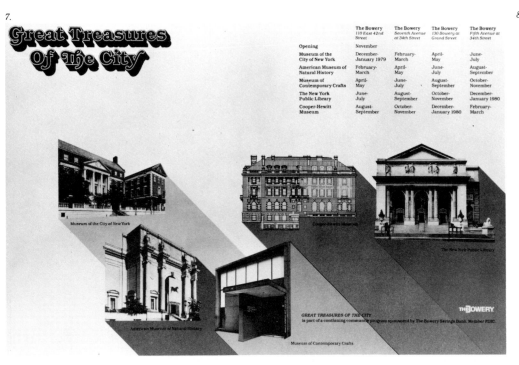

| | The Bowery<br>110 East 42nd<br>Street | The Bowery<br>Seventh Avenue<br>at 34th Street | The Bowery<br>130 Bowery at<br>Grand Street | The Bowery<br>Fifth Avenue at<br>34th Street |
|---|---|---|---|---|
| Opening | November | | | |
| Museum of the<br>City of New York | December-<br>January 1979 | February-<br>March | April-<br>May | June-<br>July |
| American Museum of<br>Natural History | February-<br>March | April-<br>May | June-<br>July | August-<br>September |
| Museum of<br>Contemporary Crafts | April-<br>May | June-<br>July | August-<br>September | October-<br>November |
| The New York<br>Public Library | June-<br>July | August-<br>September | October-<br>November | December-<br>January 1980 |
| Cooper-Hewitt<br>Museum | August-<br>September | October-<br>November | December-<br>January 1980 | February-<br>March |

Museum of the City of New York

Cooper-Hewitt Museum

The New York Public Library

American Museum of Natural History

Museum of Contemporary Crafts

GREAT TREASURES OF THE CITY
is part of a continuing community program sponsored by The Bowery Savings Bank. Member FDIC.

THE BOWERY

8.

9.

Museum of The City of New York

10.

# David Smith

Thirteen of David Smith's sculptures stood in a skylighted amphitheater at the National Gallery of Art as part of a show entitled "Subjects of the Artist." The Casebook jurors found the setting for the Smith sculptures exciting, a pleasing blend of the sculpture and its surroundings. That blend is what the National Gallery designers had striven for in the six months they worked on the assignment. Actually, the setting was not an entirely new one. In 1962, National Gallery designer Gaillard F. Ravenel saw the same 13 David Smith sculptures arranged in an amphitheater in Spoleto, Italy. Impressed, he tried to recreate the Spoleto atmosphere in the National Gallery.

Working from a ½"-scale model, the designers arranged each Smith piece precisely, adjusting the amphitheater steps and each piece's position until everything was "exactly right." They then built the full-sized amphitheater steps and platform on a framework of 4 by 4s, splicing together sections of the plywood coverings so no seams showed, and coating floor and platform with 3M's Monobase Epoxy Quartz coating, an amalgam of quartz crystals sprayed into a rolled-on epoxy resin and covered with a flat upper coating.

Quartz spotlights hanging just beneath the skylight 35' off the gallery's 3000-sq.-ft. floor picked out individual sculptures.

**Client:** National Gallery of Art (Washington, D.C.)
**Design firm:** Design Department, National Gallery of Art
**Designers:** Gaillard F. Ravenel, Mark Leithauser, Elroy Quenroe
**Fabricator:** Design and Production; Architectural Coatings (floor coating)

*1, 2. Sculptor David Smith created these 13 sculptures for an exhibit in Spoleto, Italy, where they were displayed in an amphitheater. National Gallery of Art designers recreated the feeling of that Italian amphitheater.*

2.

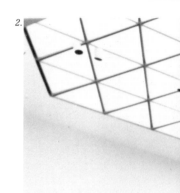

1.

# Atom Smashers...
# 50 years

The search for a way to see atoms and parts of atoms — protons, neutrons, electrons, mesons, muons, omegas, quarks — has been physics' most exciting frontier for the past 50 years. During that time most of the Nobel prizes in physics have gone to men and women working with particle accelerators, or "atom smashers," as the press and TV call them.

Within these accelerators electrical and magnetic forces excite atomic particles until they are moving so fast that they probe and disrupt atomic cores and nucleii — so fast that forces holding particles together break down, allowing particles to break up and spin off while scientists watch.

These particles are so tiny that physicists must use special and elaborate apparatus to distinguish them. One way they have of doing this is with vapor (or cloud, or bubble) chambers in which particles pass through water vapor chambers whose temperature, humidity, and pressure are so controlled that fast-moving particles leave telltale vapor trails.

"Atom Smashers...50 Years" takes visitors into the world of atomic physics. Its equipment is mammoth and expensive. Indeed, today's particle accelerators are more than a mile in diameter. Each costs hundreds of millions of dollars. And the exhibit can show only portions of them, hinting at the rest. But early particle accelerators, though large, were not too large to be brought into the 8800-sq.-ft. exhibit space on the first floor of the Smithsonian Institution's National Museum of History and Technology. In fact, one of them was built into the building as it was constructed 15

years ago. Standing in a floor well with a spiral staircase snaking around it, the 30′ high Van de Graaff accelerator built by Merle Ture in 1933 once developed a million volts, a record for its time. Electrical charges were carried into an overhead dome by a spiral conveyor belt and left there to build up. Released, the energy accelerated particles to high velocities and traces of them showed up in a vapor chamber at the accelerator's base.

These machines were pieced together by physicists, not engineers, carpenters, or architects, and they have an other-worldly look. They are, of course, the work of extraordinarily gifted, sane scientists, pursuing facts, but the machines seem mad in their juxtaposition of unusual forms, in their singular disregard for proportion and in the exuberance with which their components are jerry-rigged.

Several of these mammoth accelerators are scattered through the exhibit. Designer John Schmid and curator Dr. Paul Forman wanted visitors to have a clear understanding of the sequence in which these accelerators were developed, and thus of their historical significance. Fifty years ago, particle accelerators didn't exist; 25 years ago none was so large that it couldn't fit beneath a single roof. To establish and maintain an historical sequence, a timeline runs through the exhibit, interrupted here and there for floor space that lets visitors pass among the displays, but reappearing in front of each display. This timeline is merely a series of long, 1½″-deep boxes, raised to about waist height on metal legs. In it, beneath ½″ glass, are photos, drawings,

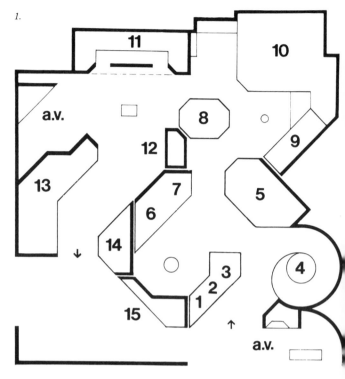

*1.*

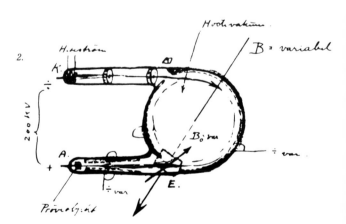

*2.*

Key:
1. Before accelerators
2. Early proposals for accelerators
3. Van de Graaff generator
4. Van de Graaff accelerator
5. Lawrence 27-inch cyclotron
6. Sixty-inch cyclotron control console
7. Kerst betatron
8. Alvarez proton linear accelerator
9. Stanford two-mile accelerator
10. McMillan synchrotron
11. Fermi 500 billion-volt synchrotron
12. Particle detectors
13. Bubble chambers
14. Current developments
15. Recent particle detectors

3.

4.

1. Plan.
2. Sketch of a particle accelerator.
3. The press reports on particle
   accelerators.
4. Exhibit entrance.
5. A time line helps visitors keep track
   of the sequence in which particle
   accelerators developed.

5.

small objects, captions, notebooks and papers that document the scientific development of particle accelerators. But the Smithsonian is not a teaching museum, and the exhibit is really an artifact exhibit, though the artifacts are outsized, even bizarre, more fantasy than artifact to someone coming on them for the first time. Still, if the show is an artifact show, it is not a quiescent one. Schmid lets visitors hear some of the sounds of these machines, their rumbling and pumping. He also uses working models. To understand the artifacts, it is necessary to know something of atom-smashing. And Schmid uses two slide shows to brief visitors about what they're seeing. One show is at the entrance, flashing a quick one-minute evolutionary history of accelerators. The second is more leisurely — 10 minutes — and gives on five screens a broader picture, ranging from the composition of the atom to the applications of nuclear research in nuclear medicine, in digital computers and in a fuller understanding of how our universe works.

Around all this Schmid created a subdued, almost mysterious, atmosphere, so that the romance and the awesomeness of what physicists have done in the past 50 years does not evaporate. Throughout he uses dark colors; and except in the entrance area, where he suspended industrial lights from the ceiling, there is no general illumination. Instead, track lighting spotlights the artifacts and interior fluorescent bulbs light the wall cases.

Positioning the mammoth artifacts required special precautions. Most of the

accelerators are mounted on platforms to distribute their weight across several floor girders and some are placed just above columns supporting the floor, in the space below. One of the show's larger pieces, a McMillan synchrotron, had been in the same space for years, shoved against a wall, resting on steel I-beams, and was too heavy to move. So Schmid had to take some space from a bookstore next door to make space for visitors to walk around the synchrotron.

Throughout, designer Schmid

alternately constricts and opens up the space to control the visitor's movement.

Since World War II, particle physics has expanded to become the dominant force in physics, and its equipment has expanded proportionally. Our largest accelerator is at the Fermi National Accelerator Laboratory in Batavia, Illinois. It is four miles in circumference and generates 500 billion volts. Schmid and Forman have recreated a 20-ft. section of the accelerator's tunnel (its housing is half submerged in the earth at

Batavia) with pipes, magnets, pumps and cables, and with photomurals at either end of the installation suggesting that the segment continues.

Though Dr. Forman worked on the "Atom Smasher" exhibit for three years, its design and installation was accomplished in 18 months on a budget of about a quarter of a million dollars. Of this sum, the Department of Energy put up some 70 per cent and in general stood behind the project, persuading laboratories across the U.S. to donate artifacts.

6. *Van de Graaff accelerator.*
7. *A mechanical device demonstrates how a cyclotron works.*
8. *Van de Graaff accelerator.*
9. *Plan view of CERN accelerator in Switzerland silk-screened on wall.*
10. *Looking into end of 17'-long section of Stanford linear accelerator.*

8.

9.

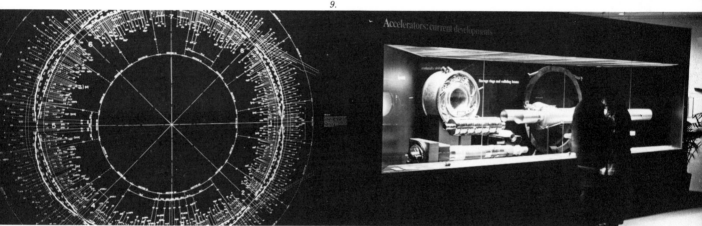

10.

**Client:** National Museum of History and Technology, Smithsonian Institution (Washington, D.C.); U.S. Department of Energy
**Design firm:** John Schmid Associates, Reston, Virginia
**Designers:** John Schmid; George Falen (detail drawings); Paul Forman, curator (Smithsonian Institution); Richard Virgo, installation manager (Smithsonian Institution); Edward Robinson, lighting design (Smithsonian Institution)
**Fabrication:** Charles M. Maltbie Associates; Production Division, Smithsonian Institution, Walter Lewis, chief.

# Airspan Display Structure

It all started because the Vetter Corporation, a West Coast manufacturer of motorcycle accessories, thought it wasn't getting enough attention at trade shows. In the previous three years the company had introduced several new products without much consumer reaction; and though Vetter had so much money invested in its modular, wooden, trade show display system that none of the company officials wanted to abandon it, clearly something had to be done. What they did was take an additional 20′ by 20′ space right next to their usual display and put up a square tent-like structure supported by air.

Needless to say, an air-supported structure is rare enough to attract attention anywhere. At a trade show its novelty is an alluring relief. But more than the structure itself attracted attention for Vetter. Through its nylon walls trade show visitors could hear faintly the sound of the slide show within, and the hint of entertainment became another lure.

If an air-supported structure seems a direct solution to Vetter's particular predicament, the road to that solution was indirect. Vetter went to Johnson Design Associates with their trade show problem, and Johnson took it to O'Riordan Designs in San Francisco. David O'Riordan had been working with airspan structures for years, experimenting with a single inflatable form for use in elementary schools, and he knew a lot about the durability and opacity of coated nylon materials. But, he says, the idea of using an airspan room at a trade show came out of talks he

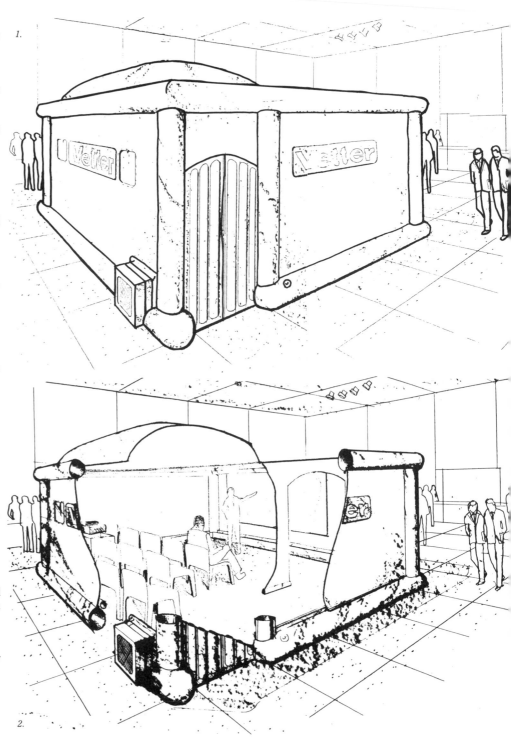

1.

2.

3.

1-3. *Supported by columns of air, this portable theater has walls held in place by Velcro fasteners. An interior blower keeps the roof from collapsing.*

had in Washington with Lee Kimche, director of the Institute for Museum Services at the Department of Health Education and Welfare, and with Michael Templeton, executive director of the Association of Science-Technology Centers. What O'Riordan was after was not just an exhibit structure that would gather a crowd. He also wanted one whose light weight would make it inexpensive to ship and easy to set up and take down.

What evolved is a 20' by 20' by 10½'-high structure that folds into a soft travel case, 5½' by 4' by 4'. Packed for shipping, it weighs just over 200 pounds.

In place, the square structure seats 20 to 25 persons for a slide show or movie. Walls are 2-oz. 130 FR Ripstop nylon, thin enough to let in some light but not so thin that the light interferes with slide viewing. These walls and the ceiling are supported by five aircells, 14" in diameter, of a tougher material, 28-oz. coated nylon, the type used in inflatable boats. A hand blower keeps the aircell tubes rigidly inflated and an interior air circulation blower creates enough interior air pressure to keep the roof from sagging (if the door is closed). It would take a deliberate knife thrust to puncture one of these aircell tubes, says David O'Riordan, and even if one were punctured the other four would hold the structure up. In any case, escape from within would be easy because the walls and ceiling are held in place merely by Velcro strip fasteners. Two men can set the whole thing up in an hour and take it down in two.

Though Vetter was the first to use the structure, Johnson Design Associates actually owns it. Johnson footed the bill for its

development and rents it to Vetter or anyone else.

Trade show-goers seem captivated by it, and O'Riordan thinks part of its appeal may be the blue color the designers chose for walls and support tubes. "Blue is cool and calming," he says, "and since the visual atmosphere at most trade shows and conventions is intense, we wanted people coming into the airspan theater to feel relaxed, cut off from the hectic pace of the convention." And Doug Johnson of Johnson Design Associates is convinced the theater pulls people. "The first time we used it," he says, "was in Anaheim on Super Bowl Sunday. There were barely 3000 people at the show; the other 10,000 were at hotels watching the game. At the convention 2000 of the people were gathered around a half dozen TV monitors. No display had any activity except the company personnel sent to run them." The Vetter booth was an exception. There, "a line of 25 people waited to see the show and many more were milling around the air structure, touching the airspan and peering in the doorway." That scene was, for Johnson, the most satisfying part of the project.

**Client:** Johnson Design Associates (San Luis Obispo, CA)
**Design firm:** O'Riordan Designs, San Francisco
**Consultant:** Ivan Swickard
**Fabricators:** Marvia Industries, (airspan frame); Narain Singh (roof and wall panels)

4.

5.

4, 5. Inside the 20' by 20' structure is room for 20 to 25 persons to watch a slide show.

# Good for Life

Though "Good for Life" is a corporate exhibit, filling the lobby of American Hospital Supply Corporation's world headquarters in Evanston, Illinois, the antecedents for its design can be found in the design of museum exhibits. American Hospital Supply wanted more than just to display its wares. (It sells some 120,000 different medical products, some of which, such as gowns and gloves, it also manufactures.) It wanted, in addition, to illustrate the development of medicine from the Stone Age to the contemporary operating room, to show how American Hospital Supply fits into that history and, by extension, into the future. So the exhibit is part education, part entertainment and part promotion.

Running through the exhibit, and serving as a physical division, is a time line, a Y-shaped table 30' long and 36' wide standing 30" off the floor. A 6"-thick plate of glass forms the top of this table, and stretching the length of the glass are six colored bands, each representing a basic area of American Hospital Supply's involvement: surgery, prosthetics, pharmacology, exploration, observation and patient care. When the stripes were silk-screened on the bottom surface of the glass, areas for photographs were masked out, then transparencies positioned in the openings. Captions in white Helvetica type are silk-screened next to the photos. What the photos and captions explain are the history of medicine. In the rest of the exhibit, American Hospital Supply makes clear its position in this historical sequence. Eight glass cases (84" high, 54" wide,

and 27" deep) hold and explain medical supplies sold by the corporation, from artificial heart valves to rubber gloves. Both cases and time line have steel-frame bases enclosed by white formica panels covered with smoked plexiglass so that they blend into the lobby's background like mist on water.

One of the most striking displays, if not the most imaginative, is a mirrored case holding row upon row of the company's disposable products: ampules, stethoscopes, forceps, scissors, etc. Another is a mannikin outfitted in medical devices. Taking an Italian clothes mannikin, the American Hospital Supply staff designers soldered him together so his joints no longer moved, and outfitted him with artificial body parts sold by the company—an artificial hand, arms, leg, false teeth, an artificial

chin. They gave him a hearing aid and an artificial lens for one eye, which glows eerily, reflecting the exhibit lights. They also cut a hole in the mannikin's chest and put in a pacemaker.

All these exhibits are static, but there is much, too, that a visitor can set in motion. A button on the pharmacology display turns on timed lights in a series of stacked boxes holding displays that illustrate the history of intravenous pharmacology. A button in the surgical display activates a film flashed on a TV screen from a tape in a room beyond the lobby, showing the teamwork and the instruments used in an operating room during surgery. Another TV-screened film shows a doctor following the progress of a catheter, by fluoroscope, as it is inserted into a patient's heart.

Less dramatic in its appeal but

*1.*

2.

3.

bolder in its concept is the use of a computer in the exhibit's patient-care section. The computer is not just *a* computer; it is *the* company computer with which American Hospital Supply keeps track of its worldwide activities. (American Hospital Supply, which has been in business for some 60 years, has 30,000 employees. Sales in 1978 were $1.74 billion.) A telephone line connects the exhibit with the computer 50 miles away, and visitors can punch a keyboard asking for information on American Hospital Supply's patient-care activities. The information appears on a screen. Giving exhibit visitors access to the company computer could pose obvious problems, but these were circumvented by blanking out most of the keyboard keys, making it possible for visitors to use only specific ones to get specific information. The readout screen also shows which hospitals in which countries are asking the

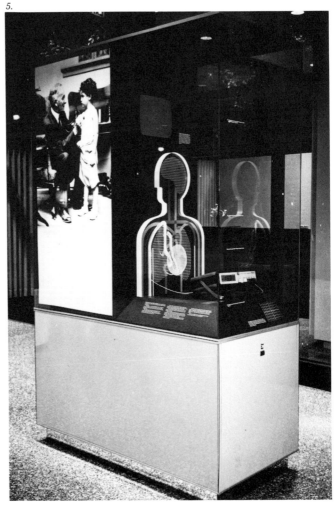

computer questions.

If the exhibit seems particularly well suited to its lobby space, it is because the designers started working with the architects two years ago as the building was being designed. Problems such as space, visitor circulation, lighting and wiring were all thought out on one drawing board.

**Client:** American Hospital Supply Corp. (Evanston, IL)
**Design firm:** American Hospital Supply Corp. design staff
**Designers:** Jeff Rich, Kerry Bierman, Tom Salisbury, David Bates (illustration), Judy Benoit (photography)
**Consultants:** Phil Smith (research-writing), Nancy Hobor (research), Cynthia Anderson Design (production art-design); Teletronic (videotapes), K&S Photographics (translites-transparencies)
**Fabricators:** Photo Impressions; Robert Peterson Design

1. A 30' long table runs through this corporate lobby exhibit, explaining through photographs (mounted beneath 6"-thick glass) American Hospital Supply's part in the history of medicine.
2, 3. Mirrored cases hold repetitive rows of the company's products.
4, 5. Other cases help explain the company's involvement in pharmacology, observation and patient care.
6. Mannikin (see also Fig. 1) is partly composed of artificial body parts sold by American Hospital Supply.

6.

The 1979 annual show of the Los Angeles Communication Arts Society (formerly the Art Directors Club of Los Angeles) was a little different. Usually, the Society has a jury which selects the best material submitted by members for display. This year, they asked each member to submit one example of his or her best work, promising to hang everything. Two hundred and eighty members submitted work, and exhibit co-chairmen Wayne Hunt and Don Clark hung all 280 examples of graphic design.

As an exhibit space they had 5000 sq. ft. of the escalator lobby in the Pacific Design Center, a huge, open, glass-enclosed space with ceilings varying in height from 8′ to 30′. Escalators poured rush-hour crowds through the exhibit. Obviously, the space created problems, no opaque walls, for instance, and too much traffic at times; but the designers' biggest problem was budget. Out of the small entrance fee they had to squeeze money not only for the exhibit's design and construction, but also for the call for entries, all advertising and promotion, an opening night party, and something, if only a mite, for the Society's operating budget.

Hunt and Clark bought some corrugated freezer cartons (6′ high and 3′ wide and deep) to use as display surfaces. Grouping these in clusters of at least four, they sliced an occasional carton in half horizontally, letting its top serve as a table for packages or looseleaf binders. Posters and other graphics were submitted with a ¼″ foam-core-board backing and were merely taped (with 3M foam tape) to the carton's corrugated sides. Hunt and Clark punched holes in the

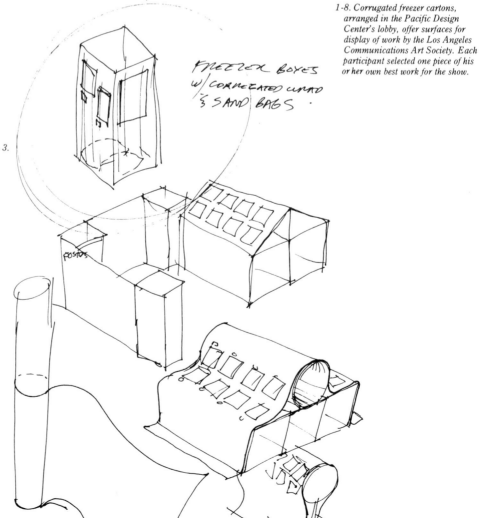

1-8. Corrugated freezer cartons, arranged in the Pacific Design Center's lobby, offer surfaces for display of work by the Los Angeles Communications Art Society. Each participant selected one piece of his or her own best work for the show.

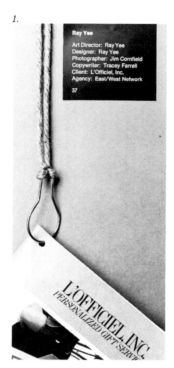

FREEZER BOXES w/ CORRUGATED WRAP & SAND BAGS.

4.

5.

corners of brochures, inserted shower curtain rings through the holes, and hung the brochures on twine from carton lips. Credits went next to each entry on negative photostats fastened to the corrugated board with spray adhesive. A single free-standing carton carried the show's titles and explanation; and hanging from the ceiling, kraft paper banners with silk-screened logos defined the space and called attention to the show. Arranging circulation was a challenge. There had to be enough space between carton groups so that visitors could stand back and look at the displays. And the exhibit couldn't crowd the escalator traffic. Hunt and Clark solved these problems by merely taking the carton tops and spending an evening trying them in different arrangements on the floor, until groupings and spaces became apparent.

The night before the opening they called on Society members, getting 20 of them to spend eight hours setting the exhibit up. Total exhibit cost — for cartons (at about $5 each), tape, twine, shower hooks, etc. — $800.

In any exhibit such as this, which relies on its content almost totally for color and form, the way the designers arrange that content is paramount. Done carefully with an eye to proportion, open space, and the proper juxtaposition of colors and angles, the show succeeds. Done indifferently, the show fails. With everything in place, this one looked handsome enough to surprise its designers.

Once the show was up, the Society had an awards judging and gave four awards. Two of them were unanimous choices: a Honda ad and the design of the show itself.

**Client:** Communication Arts Society of Los Angeles
**Designers:** Wayne Hunt, Don Clark

# Golden Treasures of Peru

Before a traveling exhibit arrives at Chicago's Field Museum of Natural History, the museum sends a curator and an exhibit designer to take a look at it in its previous installation. The reason for these inspection tours is, of course, to give the curator and the designer a basis for deciding how to adapt the exhibit to the particular confines of the Field.

Michael Moseley, the Field's assistant curator of Middle and South American archeology and ethnology, first saw the "Golden Treasures of Peru" at the American Museum of Natural History in New York where it originated. What he decided to do was to design a second exhibit to go with it.

The Field Museum has such an extensive collection of Peruvian material that Moseley envisioned an additional exhibit preparing viewers for the artifacts of Peruvian gold, an exhibit using the Field's collections to explain life in ancient Peru. Once people had an understanding of the culture that produced the gold, they would see it in a more appreciative light, he reasoned.

So the Field dug into its Peruvian collection. Designer Donald R. Skinner set up the Field's exhibit in one half of the 7380-sq.-ft. exhibit space—separated from the traveling half by a 1½′-high platform full of tropical-looking plants. One had to pass through the Field's exhibit before circling back through the traveling one: "Beautifully installed," said the Casebook jurors of the Field's display.

The museum used its own plexiglass cases, with their bases wrapped in carpet, for display of the objects and dropped existing light canopies to within 12′ of the floor beneath the 22′ ceilings.

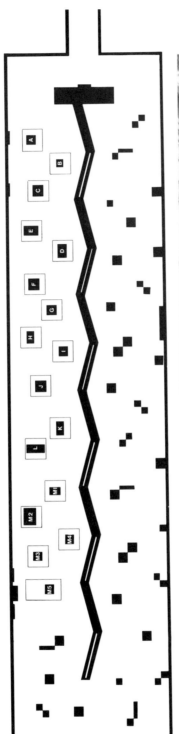

1.

2.

1. Plan shows the overall installation. Cases are outlined and lettered. Also shown is planter/panel system. Thin white lines show the hanging panels.
2. Entrance to exhibit at Field Museum.

These canopies held low-voltage
(5.5-volt) lights with lenses
specially ground to pick out
objects below with little light
spilling onto other objects or the
floor. Within each case, Skinner
positioned items carefully,
treating each case's space
three-dimensionally, "like
sculpture," filling it completely.
Plexiglass stands held many
items toward the tops of the 6′ 9″
cases. Displayed were fabrics,
pottery, burial garments, and
stone tools used in working gold
(the latter supplied by Boston's
Peabody Museum). Photomurals
(taken from the same source as
those used in the traveling part of
the show), 8′ high and 12′ wide,
suspended above the floor and
segmented like Chinese screens,
show Peru as it was at the time of
the Spanish conquest. These
photomurals stood out against
the dark brown walls and the
gray-brown carpet. Typefaces
were Korinna, to match that in
the traveling exhibit.

The Field put its exhibit
together in three months on a
design budget of about $15,000.

3. *Exhibit symbol.*
4-6. *Field Museum dug into its own
Peruvian collection to add to a
traveling exhibit of Peruvian gold.
The museum divided its collection
from the traveling one by a strip of
plants, and displayed its artifacts in
existing vitrines with carpet-wrapped
bases.*

**Client:** Field Museum of Natural
History (Chicago)
**Design firm:** Department of
Exhibition, Field Museum of Natural
History
**Designer:** Donald R. Skinner
**Fabricators:** Tesko Welding; Dave
Kleiman Studios: Field Museum of
Natural History

3.

4.

# Overglaze Imagery, Cone 019-016

OVERGLAZE IMAGERY
Cone 019-016

"An object lesson in how to install a show," said the Casebook jurors of this exhibit, which ran for a little over a month in the Art Gallery of California State University in Fullerton. Consisting of 180 ceramic objects, it was arranged in three sections: Painted Porcelain and Faience, 13th Century – Early 20th Century; World of the China Painter, Late 19th-20th Century; and Beyond the Barriers of Tradition, Late 20th Century. Within the exhibit, two small theaters (holding four 8' benches) showed continuous slide shows: one of the history of overglaze porcelain painting; and one dealing with the contemporary women who make up the world of 20th-century overglaze painting. Both shows illustrate techniques of overglaze painting and the low-intensity kiln firing that hardens it. More immediate but less frequent were occasional lectures on and actual demonstrations of china painting held in space next to the 2600-sq.-ft. exhibit gallery.

But what the jurors meant when they spoke of the installation as an object lesson were neither the live demonstrations nor the audio-visual programs. Their praise was for the way the artifacts—vases, plates, platters and other ceramic objects— were displayed. Gallery director Dextra Frankel, whose design firm, LA.X Studios, designed the installation, made certain that each piece seemed to stand alone, that each had enough individually defined space to stand out regardless of its size or shape. Several techniques ensured this space and definition. Though most of the items were displayed in horizontal plexiglass-fronted cases, 8' long and 18"

*1-9. "Overglaze Imagery" exhibit was mounted in 8'-long horizontal cases. Within these cases each piece was given definition and distinction by the way it was positioned.*

4.

high and deep, Frankel and her co-designer, Thomas Hartman, isolated each piece by raising it slightly on its own platform or slanted display board, or in some cases, by partitioning it from its neighbors. In at least one instance, the designers have a tureen resting on a plexiglass box above a mirror to expose the tureen's glazed underside. Hartman designed a series of modular display platforms to raise each artifact off the display case's floor or to hold it out from the case's back wall.

Frankel is articulate about the instincts she follows in positioning items in a show such as this. She will not, for instance, group objects with similar textures, judging that to do so makes them run together. And she tries to avoid grouping objects of the same shape, preferring to give a viewer's eye, moving through the exhibit, constant variety or surprise. She has, in some instances, alternated objects placed on platforms on the floor of the cases with objects mounted on the cases' back walls. Never, she says, mount an object directly on the floor; it will seem heavy there, even clumsy, as if tethered awkwardly. If, instead, artifacts are raised slightly on a platform, they will, she maintains, appear to float.

The CSUF Art Gallery exhibit space is partitioned by a movable wall system developed for other shows; and the cases, designed specially for this show, have lips that let them attach readily to the wall system. Built of scrap plywood, the cases screw together, and in the top of each is a light-diffusing panel, held in place by the plexiglass panel that is the case's front. Lighting within each case comes from

5.

6.

Light-O-Lier track fixtures, modified to hold 150-watt bulbs, suspended in rows of four within the walls, 30″ above a diffuser panel in each display case's top. Everything within the case is thus lighted evenly.

Ambient illumination in the gallery comes from standard track lighting. These lights play off the painted walls, which designer Tom Hartman describes as a "grayed" rose color, a Pratt and Lambert color chosen because its transparency makes it seem as if the color "resides deep beneath the surface," the way color does in good porcelain. In the entrance hallway and the slide show area walls are a Pratt and Lambert deep purple.

Frankel and Hartman put the exhibit together in two months on a budget of $28,000, part of which came from the National Endowment for the Arts. Included in the budget was design and production of a 206-page catalogue.

**Client:** Art Gallery, Visual Arts Center, California State University, Fullerton; Dextra Frankel, director.
**Design firm:** LA.X studios, Laguna Beach, CA
**Designers:** Dextra Frankel, Thomas Hartman
**Consultants:** Jerry Samuelson, Daniel Stearns, Amy Nagasawa, catalogue design; Mark Schwartz, catalogue photography; Garth Clark, Judy Chicago, audio-visual presentation in consultation with Museum Studies Program, CSUF
**Fabrication:** Art Gallery Staff, CSUF

7.

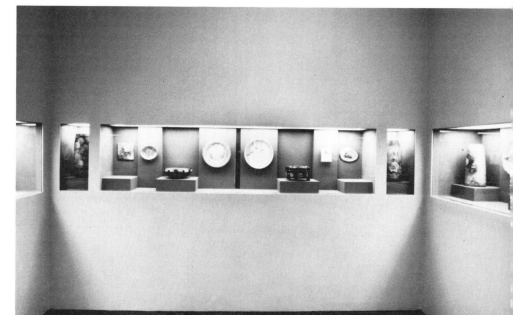
8.

9.